INCREDIBLE

One-Pot

Cooking

Easy, Delicious Recipes for Exciting Meals—Without the Mess

MEGAN MARLOWE

Creator of Strawberry Blondie Kitchen

PAGE STREET
PUBLISHING CO.

PAGE STREET
PUBLISHING CO.

First published in 2020 by
Page Street Publishing Co.
27 Congress Street, Suite 105
Salem, MA 01970
www.pagestreetpublishing.com

Distributed by Macmillan, sales in Canada by The Canadian Manda Group.

24 23 22 21 20   1 2 3 4 5

ISBN-13: 978-1-62414-974-0
ISBN-10: 1-62414-974-X

Library of Congress Control Number: 2019942855

Cover and book design by Rosie Stewart for Page Street Publishing Co.
Photography by Megan Marlowe

Printed and bound in the United States

Page Street Publishing protects our planet by donating to nonprofits like The Trustees, which focuses on local land conservation.

TO MY FAMILY

Jim, Aiden, Chloe and Dad

TABLE OF
Contents

INTRODUCTION

As a busy mom of two children, I know how hard it can be to get dinner on the table. Between working, after-school activities and homework, who has time for complicated recipes? Easy, quick, approachable—and most importantly—delicious recipes have become my go-to staples, and if they can be cooked in one vessel, even better.

It wasn't until I was 22 years old that I became really interested in cooking. After watching Rachael Ray make her 30-minute meals, I purchased my first Magic Bullet Blender and tried to whip up some fettuccine Alfredo with my sister. After that, I began to forge my path and find my own style of cooking: easy, approachable meals without the mess.

I began my food blog, Strawberry Blondie Kitchen, in 2015 after encouragement from my husband to start documenting the recipes I was making in the kitchen. Now here I am, sharing these one-pot/one-pan recipes with you (in a book!) so that you can spend less time doing the dishes and more quality time with the ones you love.

My mission with this cookbook is to save you from scrambling for more than one pan, dish or pot while preparing a delicious dinner. After all, who has time for all the cleanup? Another added timesaving bonus: many of these meals take just 30 minutes or less to come together. You'll also notice I've taken beloved, traditional meals and put my own spin on them to create something new and different. Out with the same old dull recipes and in with new, reimagined flavors the whole family will enjoy!

If you are someone who finds themself throwing together the same meal week after week in an effort to save time in the kitchen, you'll love these recipes. They're far from boring and require minimal effort. Having once been a novice cook myself, I understand how hard it can be to approach a recipe and not really know where to start. The recipes in this book are far from complicated, and they don't require crazy ingredients lists or a multitude of cooking methods. I want to make you feel like the MVP in your kitchen without having to stress.

I hope these recipes inspire you to get into the kitchen and bring you nostalgia, laughter and a new favorite dish, without all the fuss of cleanup time!

Megan Marlowe

COOP'D UP IN
One Pan

I don't know about you, but I love a quick and delicious chicken dish. Sometimes, though, I get tired of eating the same recipes over and over again. I can only eat chicken parmesan so many times before I vow never to touch it again. So, in this chapter, I've taken those classic chicken recipes you may have grown up with and given them a flavorful twist to save you from the dreaded dinner rut. Don't save chicken cordon bleu for a special occasion. On page 16, it gets combined with meatloaf for a comforting dish that's suitable for any night of the week. And on page 19, walking tacos get an upgrade with the addition of buffalo chicken. In this chapter, there's enough variety to tantalize everyone's taste buds. And the best part? All of the recipes are cooked in just one pan, pot or dish. Say goodbye to hours of standing at the kitchen sink and sulking while doing all of those dishes. Winner, winner, it's chicken for dinner!

Chicken with Herb and Onion Dumplings

Nothing says comfort more than a big bowl of chicken and dumplings. While I was never fortunate enough to eat my grandmother's dumplings, her children rave about them. A quick browse through her beloved recipes and lo and behold, I had the treasured dumpling recipe. Of course, I had to make it my own with the addition of dill, which pairs beautifully with chicken. These dumplings are light, fluffy and the perfect topping for the creamy chicken mixture.

SERVES 4

CHICKEN

2 tbsp (30 ml) olive oil

6 (4-oz [112-g]) boneless, skinless chicken thighs

1½ tsp (8 g) salt, divided

1 tsp black pepper, divided

4 tbsp (60 g) butter

1 medium yellow onion, diced

3 medium carrots, peeled and diced

3 medium ribs celery, coarsely chopped

2 cloves garlic, minced

4 sprigs fresh thyme or 1 tsp dried thyme

¼ cup (30 g) all-purpose flour

4 cups (960 ml) chicken stock

1 dried bay leaf

1 cup (240 ml) milk

DUMPLINGS

1 cup (90 g) cake flour

2 tsp (8 g) double-acting baking powder

½ tsp salt

1 large egg, beaten

¼ cup (60 ml) milk, plus more as needed

1 tbsp (3 g) minced fresh parsley, plus more for garnish

1 tbsp (3 g) minced fresh dill, plus more for garnish

1 tbsp (13 g) grated onion

To make the chicken, heat the oil in a large, heavy-bottomed pot over medium-high heat.

Season the chicken thighs all over with 1 teaspoon of the salt and ½ teaspoon of the black pepper. Place the thighs in the pot and cook until brown, 2 to 3 minutes. Flip the thighs and cook for 2 to 3 minutes, or until brown. Transfer the chicken to a plate.

Add the butter, onion, carrots, celery and garlic to the pot and sauté until they are soft, about 5 minutes. Add the remaining ½ teaspoon of salt, ½ teaspoon of black pepper and thyme. Sprinkle in the all-purpose flour. Cook for 1 minute, until the mixture is smooth.

Slowly add the stock, scraping up the browned bits on the bottom of the pot. Add the bay leaf.

Bring the mixture to a boil, then reduce the heat to medium-low and add the milk and chicken. Simmer the mixture for 20 to 25 minutes, or until the chicken is cooked through.

Meanwhile, make the dumplings. In a medium bowl, sift the cake flour, baking powder and salt three times. Add the egg and milk and stir until the mixture is just combined. If the dough isn't coming together, add more milk, 1 teaspoon at a time, but note that you want the mixture to be stiff. Add the parsley, dill and onion.

When the chicken is cooked, remove it from the pot to cool. When it's cool enough to handle, shred it and transfer it back to the pot.

To cook the dumplings, scoop 1½-tablespoon (23-g) balls of the dough and add them to the pot. You should have approximately 12 dumplings. Cover the pot and simmer the chicken and dumplings for 15 minutes, until the dumplings are light and fluffy. Discard the bay leaf.

Place the chicken mixture into 4 bowls and top each serving with 3 or 4 dumplings. Garnish with the additional parsley and dill.

*See photo on page 8.

Loaded Tortilla-Crusted Chicken Finger Nachos

Nothing gets my kids to the dinner table faster than chicken fingers, so imagine how fast they came running when I topped those chicken fingers with cheese and all their favorite nacho toppings. When it's nacho night, don't be the last one to the table!

SERVES 4

CHICKEN FINGERS

1½ lbs (675 g) chicken breast tenderloins

1 tsp salt

½ tsp black pepper

½ cup (60 g) all-purpose flour

2 large eggs, beaten

2 cups (125 g) crushed tortilla chips, any variety

1 cup (120 g) shredded Cheddar cheese

½ cup (65 g) shredded Monterey Jack cheese

PICO DE GALLO

3 medium Roma tomatoes, finely chopped

¼ cup (38 g) red onion, diced

1 jalapeño, seeded and finely chopped

2 tbsp (6 g) finely chopped fresh cilantro

OPTIONAL TOPPINGS

Coarsely chopped avocado

Sliced black olives

Sliced jalapeños

To make the chicken fingers, preheat the oven to 400°F (204°C) and spray a 12 x 17–inch (30 x 43–cm) baking sheet with cooking spray.

Sprinkle the chicken with the salt and black pepper.

Set up a breading station with 3 shallow dishes; add the flour to the first, the eggs to the second and the tortilla chips to the third.

Dip each chicken tender into the flour, then into the eggs and finally into the tortilla chips, making sure to coat all sides of the chicken. Place the chicken tenders on the prepared baking sheet.

Bake the chicken tenders for 10 minutes; then, flip them and bake for 10 minutes.

Meanwhile, make the pico de gallo. In a medium bowl, combine the tomatoes, onion, jalapeño and cilantro. Set aside.

Remove the chicken tenders from the oven and sprinkle them with the Cheddar and Monterey Jack cheeses. Bake them for 2 to 3 minutes, or until the cheeses are melted.

Sprinkle the chicken tenders with the pico de gallo and any of the optional toppings before serving.

Jalapeño Popper Chicken Burgers

Jalapeño poppers was one of the first recipes I ever made on my blog, so they hold a special place in my heart and in my belly. My husband and I like things spicy, but we also have small children who do not. Therefore, I remove the seeds and the ribs from the jalapeños—that way, they aren't too spicy but still contribute some heat to the dish. These burgers are paired with cream cheese and two types of Cheddar cheese, and they've quickly become a family staple. (In fact, they're tied for second with my husband's favorite recipe in this book, Chili Mac Tortilla Pie [page 93].) If you aren't a fan of spicy foods, feel free to sub the jalapeños with poblano peppers for a milder taste.

SERVES 4

2 oz (56 g) cream cheese

1 medium jalapeño, seeded and diced

2 tbsp (14 g) bacon bits or cooked and crumbled bacon

¼ cup (30 g) shredded Cheddar cheese

1 lb (450 g) ground chicken breast

1 tsp salt

½ tsp black pepper

¼ cup (14 g) panko breadcrumbs

2 tbsp (30 ml) olive oil

4 slices sharp Cheddar cheese

4 lettuce leaves

4 hamburger buns

In a medium bowl, combine the cream cheese, jalapeño, bacon bits and shredded Cheddar cheese.

In a large bowl, combine the chicken, salt, black pepper and breadcrumbs.

Evenly form the chicken mixture into 4 (4¼-ounce [119-g]) portions. Make a well in the center of each ball of meat and place 1 tablespoon (15 g) of the cream cheese mixture into the center. Form the patty around the mixture, completely enclosing it.

Heat the oil in a medium skillet over medium-high heat. Add the burgers and cook them for 5 to 6 minutes per side, until lightly browned.

During the last minute of cooking, add 1 slice of the sharp Cheddar cheese on top of each burger and allow it to melt.

To serve, place the lettuce on the bottom of each hamburger bun and top with a jalapeño popper burger.

Chicken Cordon Bleu Meatloaf

My family loves super cheesy meatloaf—and I'm a big fan of having few to no dishes during cleanup! This chicken cordon bleu meatloaf is no exception on either front: It's packed full of tangy Swiss cheese, sharp Dijon mustard and smoky ham to bring you a meatloaf no one will refuse, all in just one loaf pan.

SERVES 4

1 lb (450 g) ground chicken

2 cloves garlic, minced

½ cup (28 g) panko breadcrumbs

4 oz (112 g) smoked deli ham, coarsely chopped

4 oz (112 g) Swiss cheese, grated

¼ cup (38 g) diced yellow onion

1 medium egg

½ tsp salt

½ tsp dried parsley

¼ tsp black pepper

3 tbsp (45 g) Dijon mustard, divided

Preheat the oven to 400°F (204°C). Spray a 9 x 5–inch (23 x 13–cm) loaf pan with cooking spray.

In a large bowl, mix the chicken, garlic, breadcrumbs, ham, Swiss cheese, onion, egg, salt, parsley, black pepper and 2 tablespoons (30 g) of the mustard. Add the chicken mixture to the prepared loaf pan.

Spread the remaining 1 tablespoon (15 g) of mustard over the top of the meatloaf.

Bake the meatloaf for 40 to 45 minutes, until the center is set and the top is golden brown. Allow it to cool slightly before slicing and serving.

Buffalo Chicken Walking Tacos

This recipe is a mash-up for the books. My family loves tacos, but I like to make mealtime more fun by serving them straight out of corn chip bags with some forks. Less mess and less cleanup for me! I took those classic walking tacos and upgraded them with chicken that's simmered in buffalo sauce then topped with blue cheese, cilantro, a drizzle of ranch and a few slices of jalapeños for some extra spice.

SERVES 4

2 tbsp (30 ml) olive oil

2 (8-oz [224-g]) boneless, skinless chicken breasts, cut into ½-inch (13-mm) cubes

½ tsp salt

¼ tsp black pepper

2 medium ribs celery, coarsely chopped

2 medium carrots, peeled and diced

⅓ cup (80 ml) buffalo sauce

2 oz (56 g) cream cheese

4 (1-oz [28-g]) bags corn chips

Ranch dressing (optional)

Blue cheese (optional)

Sliced jalapeños (optional)

Heat the oil in a medium skillet over medium heat. Add the chicken, season with the salt and black pepper and cook for 5 to 6 minutes.

Add the celery and carrots and sauté for 2 minutes. Stir in the buffalo sauce and cream cheese and cook until the cream cheese melts, about 2 minutes.

Slice open each bag of corn chips and spoon the filling on top of the chips.

If desired, top the walking tacos with the ranch dressing, blue cheese and jalapeños.

Barbecue Chicken Casserole with Jalapeño-Cheddar Cornbread

One of my must-have side dishes at any barbecue meal is cornbread. As I was cooking this casserole, I wondered, how can I have both in this one-skillet meal? Easy! Top the whole thing with cornbread. Now I can have all of my favorites in one skillet!

SERVES 6

BARBECUE CHICKEN

1 lb (450 g) boneless, skinless chicken breasts, diced into ½-inch (13-mm) cubes

4 slices bacon, coarsely chopped

1 small yellow onion, diced

1 medium green bell pepper, coarsely chopped

2 cloves garlic, minced

1½ cups (360 ml) barbecue sauce

1 (15-oz [420-g]) can pinto beans, drained and rinsed

1 tsp salt

1 tsp smoked paprika

¼ tsp black pepper

JALAPEÑO-CHEDDAR CORNBREAD

1 (8½-oz [238-g]) box cornbread mix

1 large egg

⅓ cup (80 ml) milk

¾ cup (90 g) shredded Cheddar cheese

1 medium jalapeño, diced

Preheat the oven to 400°F (204°C).

To make the barbecue chicken, heat a medium oven-safe skillet over medium heat. Add the chicken and bacon and cook for 8 to 10 minutes, until the chicken is no longer pink. Add the onion, bell pepper and garlic and sauté for 5 minutes, until the vegetables are soft.

Add the barbecue sauce, pinto beans, salt, smoked paprika and black pepper and stir to combine. Cook the casserole for 5 minutes, so that the flavors can come together.

Meanwhile, make the jalapeño-Cheddar cornbread. In a medium bowl, stir together the cornbread mix, egg, milk, cheese and jalapeño.

Evenly spread the cornbread batter on top of the casserole mixture.

Place the skillet in the oven and bake the casserole for 20 minutes, or until the cornbread is light brown around the edges. Slice the casserole into 6 pieces and serve.

Everything but the Bagel Avocado Chicken

The hottest thing to hit the foodie scene in the past few years has been avocado toast. Let's take that one step further and put that delicious avocado spread on top of breaded chicken. You can choose to top your avocado chicken with sliced hard-boiled eggs, a bruschetta mixture or some everything bagel seasoning. Heck, you could even leave it plain, it's that good. Welcome to the world, Everything but the Bagel Avocado Chicken . . . let's make it a thing!

SERVES 4

CHICKEN

½ cup (60 g) all-purpose flour

¾ tsp salt

½ tsp black pepper

½ tsp paprika

2 large eggs

1 cup (55 g) panko breadcrumbs

2 tbsp (20 g) Everything but the Bagel seasoning

4 (4-oz [112-g]) chicken cutlets

AVOCADO TOPPING

2 medium avocados

1 clove garlic, minced

Salt, as needed

Black pepper, as needed

OPTIONAL TOPPINGS

Sliced hard-boiled eggs

Bruschetta topping

To make the chicken, preheat the oven to 400°F (204°C). Spray a 12 x 17–inch (30 x 43–cm) baking sheet with cooking spray.

In a shallow dish, stir together the flour, salt, black pepper and paprika. In a second shallow dish, whisk the eggs. In a third shallow dish, stir together the breadcrumbs and seasoning.

Dip each chicken cutlet into the flour mixture, then into the eggs and finally into the breadcrumbs. Place the cutlets on the prepared baking sheet.

Bake the chicken for 30 minutes, or until the chicken's internal temperature reaches 165°F (74°C).

While the chicken bakes, make the avocado topping. In a small bowl, mash the avocados and add the garlic, salt and black pepper. Stir to combine.

Before serving, spread the avocado mixture on the chicken, and top the chicken with the hard-boiled eggs and bruschetta (if using).

Charcuterie Board Stuffed Chicken

Whenever my girlfriend Mel and I get together, we enjoy putting out a pretty epic cheese board (at least we think it's epic, anyway). A few favorites we always include are olive tapenade, Brie and salami. "Why not stuff all of those delicious charcuterie board ingredients into a chicken breast?" Mel said one day. Genius!

SERVES 4

4 (4-oz [112-g]) chicken cutlets

Salt, as needed

Black pepper, as needed

8 slices Genoa salami

½ cup (90 g) olive tapenade

4 rectangular slices Brie cheese, without rind

2 tbsp (30 ml) olive oil

Side salad, vegetables or French bread, for serving

Preheat the oven to 350°F (177°C). Season the chicken with the salt and black pepper.

Place 2 slices of the salami on each chicken cutlet; then top the salami with 2 tablespoons (23 g) of the olive tapenade and 1 slice of the cheese. Roll the chicken around the filling, tucking the filling in as you work. Use toothpicks to secure the chicken.

Heat the oil in a large, oven-safe skillet over medium-high heat. Add the chicken to the skillet and cook on each side for 3 to 4 minutes, or until it's golden brown.

Transfer the skillet to the oven and bake for 10 to 15 minutes, or until the chicken's internal temperature reaches 165°F (74°C).

Transfer the chicken to individual plates and serve it with a side salad, vegetables or sliced French bread.

Nashville Hot Cobb Salad

Since Nashville hot chicken hit the scene, nothing is safe, not even Cobb salad. I know that Nashville hot chicken is typically fried, but frying defeats the purpose of eating a salad, so my version is baked. I promise you won't miss the frying. Serve this salad with your favorite dressing—personally, I'm partial to ranch, since it's delicious and cools my mouth at the same time.

SERVES 4

⅓ cup (40 g) all-purpose flour

2 tsp (6 g) chili powder

1½ tsp (5 g) cayenne pepper

1 tsp dark brown sugar

1 tsp smoked paprika

1 tsp ground cumin

1 tsp garlic powder

1 tsp onion powder

1 tsp salt

1 tsp black pepper

2 large eggs

½ cup (28 g) panko breadcrumbs

4 (8-oz [224-g]) boneless, skinless chicken breasts

6 slices bacon

4 medium romaine hearts, coarsely chopped

4 large hard-boiled eggs, diced

2 medium avocados, diced

5 oz (140 g) cherry tomatoes, halved

4 oz (112 g) blue cheese, crumbled

Salad dressing of choice, for serving

Preheat the oven to 400°F (204°C) and spray a 12 x 17–inch (30 x 43–cm) baking sheet with cooking spray.

In a shallow dish, stir the flour, chili powder, cayenne pepper, brown sugar, smoked paprika, cumin, garlic powder, onion powder, salt and black pepper. In a second shallow dish, whisk the eggs. Place the breadcrumbs in a third shallow dish.

Dip each chicken breast into the flour, then dip it into the eggs and finally into the breadcrumbs. Arrange the chicken breasts on one side of the prepared baking sheet. Place the bacon on the other side of the baking sheet.

Bake the chicken and bacon for 20 to 25 minutes, or until the chicken's internal temperature reaches 165°F (74°C). Remove the baking sheet from the oven and allow everything to cool slightly. Slice each chicken breast into ½-inch (13-mm) thick strips and crumble the bacon.

While the chicken and bacon cool, place the romaine lettuce into a large bowl. Arrange each ingredient in its own respective row on top of the lettuce: hard-boiled eggs, avocados, bacon, chicken, tomatoes and blue cheese.

Serve the salad with the salad dressing of your choice.

Chicken Surprise with Baby Potatoes

When I was growing up, my mother would make this dish called chicken surprise. It was a chicken breast topped with bacon and smothered in a white cream sauce. I decided to re-create the dish because it was one of my favorite meals growing up. I put my own spin on this beloved dish by stuffing the chicken breasts with pimento cheese and wrapping them in bacon. Add a side of roasted potatoes and you'll have a new favorite meal for your dinner rotation.

SERVES 4

BABY POTATOES

1½ lbs (675 g) mixed baby potatoes, quartered

1 tbsp (15 ml) olive oil

½ tsp salt

½ tsp black pepper

CHICKEN

2 oz (56 g) room-temperature cream cheese

1 tbsp (14 g) mayonnaise

2 tbsp (22 g) jarred diced pimento peppers

⅛ tsp garlic powder

⅛ tsp onion powder

⅛ tsp red pepper flakes (optional)

4 (4-oz [112-g]) chicken cutlets

½ tsp salt

4 slices bacon

Preheat the oven to 400°F (204°C) and spray a 12 x 17–inch (30 x 43–cm) baking sheet with cooking spray.

To make the baby potatoes, place the potatoes in a large bowl and toss them with the oil, salt and black pepper. Arrange them on one side of the prepared baking sheet.

To make the chicken, combine the cream cheese, mayonnaise, pimento peppers, garlic powder, onion powder and red pepper flakes (if using) in a medium bowl.

Season both sides of the chicken with the salt.

Spread 1 tablespoon (15 g) of the pimento cheese over the surface of each chicken cutlet and roll up the chicken. Wrap a slice of bacon around each chicken cutlet and secure it with a few toothpicks. Place the chicken on the prepared baking sheet.

Bake the chicken and baby potatoes for 25 minutes, or until the potatoes are golden brown. Place the chicken on individual plates and evenly distribute the potatoes among them.

Jerk Lettuce Wraps with Peanut Sauce

Some people can eat ketchup on anything, but my family could drizzle peanut sauce on everything. Salad, pasta, Peanut Butter and Jelly Wings (page 32)—you name it, nothing is off-limits in this family. The sauce in this recipe is simple to prepare at home, so skip the premade version and do it yourself.

SERVES 4

PEANUT SAUCE

¾ cup (135 g) chunky peanut butter

¾ cup (180 ml) full-fat canned coconut milk

3 tbsp (36 g) sugar

2 tbsp (30 ml) soy sauce

2 cloves garlic, minced

1 tbsp (15 g) minced fresh ginger

2 tsp (10 ml) toasted sesame oil

Juice of ½ lime

LETTUCE WRAPS

2 tbsp (30 ml) olive oil

4 (4-oz [112-g]) boneless, skinless chicken breasts

1 tbsp (9 g) jerk seasoning

8 leaves butter lettuce

3 green onions, minced

½ cup (25 g) shredded carrots

To make the peanut sauce, stir together the peanut butter, coconut milk, sugar, soy sauce, garlic, ginger, sesame oil and lime juice in a medium bowl. Set the peanut sauce aside.

To make the lettuce wraps, heat the olive oil in a large skillet over medium heat. Season both sides of the chicken with the jerk seasoning. Add the chicken and cook until it is golden brown and cooked through, 4 to 5 minutes on each side. Transfer the chicken to a plate to cool. When the chicken is cool enough to handle, dice it.

To serve, place 1 to 2 tablespoons (9 to 18 g) of the chicken into each lettuce leaf; then drizzle each lettuce cup with 1 tablespoon (15 ml) of the peanut sauce. Sprinkle the lettuce cups with the green onions and carrots.

Peanut Butter and Jelly Wings

My sister told us about this amazing wing place by her house and said that we'd have to try the PB&J wings. Hesitantly, we ordered them—and our lives would never be the same. The wings were crispy and bursting with sweet peanut butter and jelly flavors. I went home to recreate those wings, which are perfect for serving during a football game when you have a house full of people—and now we can save a two-hour drive to the wing place that started this love affair.

SERVES 8

PEANUT BUTTER AND JELLY SAUCE

¾ cup (135 g) chunky peanut butter

¾ cup (180 ml) canned coconut milk

3 tbsp (36 g) sugar

2 tbsp (30 ml) soy sauce

2 cloves garlic, minced

1 tbsp (15 g) minced fresh ginger

2 tsp (10 ml) toasted sesame oil

Juice of ½ lime

½ cup (163 g) grape jelly or jelly of choice

WINGS

3 lbs (1.4 kg) frozen chicken wings, defrosted

2 tbsp (24 g) aluminum-free baking powder

1 tsp salt

Preheat the oven to 350°F (177°C) and place a wire cooling rack, sprayed with cooking spray, inside a 12 x 17–inch (30 x 43–cm) baking sheet.

To make the peanut butter and jelly sauce, combine the peanut butter, coconut milk, sugar, soy sauce, garlic, ginger, sesame oil, lime juice and jelly in a medium bowl. Set the sauce aside.

To make the wings, toss the wings with the baking powder and salt in a large bowl.

Place the wings on the prepared baking sheet and bake for 30 minutes. Increase the oven temperature to 425°F (218°C) and bake the wings for 15 minutes.

Transfer the wings to a large bowl. Toss the wings in two-thirds of the peanut butter and jelly sauce and return them to the baking sheet. Bake for 15 minutes.

Serve the wings with the remaining one-third of the peanut butter and jelly sauce.

Chicks in a Blanket

My kids love anything wrapped in a "blanket." But instead of using
a regular hot dog, I decided to use our favorite tomato-basil chicken
sausages. These wrapped sausages are fun to make, and even the kids
enjoy helping prepare them for dinner. We like to serve these alongside
French fries to round out the meal. Feel free to use any
variety of sausage and cheese you'd like.

SERVES 4

HOMEMADE PESTO

2 cups (48 g) fresh basil leaves, stems removed

¼ cup (34 g) pine nuts or walnuts

3 cloves garlic

¼ tsp salt

¼ tsp black pepper

½ cup (90 g) freshly grated Parmesan or Pecorino Romano cheese

½ cup (120 ml) extra-virgin olive oil

CHICKS IN A BLANKET

2 tbsp (22 g) grated Parmesan cheese

2 tbsp (6 g) Italian seasoning

1 (8-oz [224-g]) container crescent roll dough (such as Pillsbury™ Butter Flake Crescent Rolls)

4 slices mozzarella cheese, cut in half

1 (12-oz [336-g]) package fully cooked tomato-basil chicken sausages, cut in half

To make the homemade pesto, combine the basil, pine nuts, garlic, salt, black pepper and Parmesan cheese in a food processor. Pulse 5 to 10 times. Then, with the food processor running, slowly stream in the oil. Set the pesto aside.

To make the chicks in a blanket, preheat the oven to 375°F (191°C) and spray a 12 x 17–inch (30 x 43–cm) baking sheet with cooking spray.

In a small bowl, combine the Parmesan cheese and Italian seasoning. Set the bowl aside.

Unroll the crescent roll dough and divide it into individual triangles. Place a piece of mozzarella cheese on the widest end of a triangle. Top each piece of cheese with a sausage half and roll up the dough. Place the chick in a blanket on the prepared baking sheet.

Sprinkle the chicks in a blanket with the Parmesan cheese mixture and bake them for 10 to 12 minutes, until they are a light golden brown.

Serve the chicks in a blanket with the homemade pesto for dipping.

MEATY CLASSICS WITH Easy Cleanup

After you prepare the recipes in this chapter, no one will have to fight over whose turn it is to wash the dishes because only one pan, dish or pot is needed for these beef, pork and turkey recipes.

My husband is a meat-and-potatoes kind of guy, but even that can get a little boring each and every night for dinner. So I took some of his favorite dishes, such as schnitzel, and put my own spin on them. Check out my Pork Rind Schnitzel on page 39. It's a crispier take on the classic—and don't forget the applesauce!

The recipes in this chapter add a little pizzazz to your normal routine. The kids will love my grandmother's take on tacos with Poor Man Taco's on page 44. And if you're looking for a hearty comfort meal, the Sheet Pan Italian Pepper Mini Meatloaves (page 43) will completely satisfy you.

For some major nostalgia, there's my Deluxe Cheeseburger Sloppy Joes on page 53, which the entire family will gobble up. That recipe is everything you love about a cheeseburger but in sloppy Joe form and piled high with your favorite burger toppings.

Pork Rind Schnitzel

When I met my husband, I was first introduced to schnitzel: thin pork chops coated in saltine crackers (which is how his grandmother made it; I now make it with beef). Fast-forward fourteen years later and he's on the Keto diet. How can I still make our family's favorite dish but keep it diet-friendly for the hubs? Pork rinds, that's how. Pork rinds make for a crispy piece of meat that's delicious and still must be topped with applesauce.

SERVES 6

Vegetable oil, as needed

6 (4-oz [112-g]) cube steaks, pounded ½-inch (13-mm) thick

1 tsp salt

½ tsp black pepper

½ cup (60 g) all-purpose flour

2 large eggs, beaten

1 cup (32 g) finely crushed pork rinds

Applesauce, for serving

Preheat the oven to 250°F (121°C). Place a 10 x 16–inch (25 x 40–cm) wire rack inside a 12 x 17–inch (30 x 43–cm) baking sheet.

Add enough oil to a large, shallow pan so the oil comes up the sides of the pan about one-fourth of the way. Set the pan over medium heat.

Sprinkle the cubed steak with the salt and black pepper.

Set up a breading station with 3 shallow dishes: the flour in the first dish, the eggs in the second and the pork rinds in the third.

Dip the cube steak in the flour, shaking off any excess, then dip it in the eggs, allowing any excess to drip off. Then dip the steak in the pork rinds, pressing to make sure they adhere to the meat.

Place the steaks in the pan and pan-fry until they're golden brown, 3 to 4 minutes per side.

Transfer the cooked steaks to the prepared baking sheet and place it in the oven to keep the steaks warm until all the steaks are cooked.

Serve the schnitzel with the applesauce.

Apple Stuffed Turkey Burgers

This is a shout-out to my girl, Rachael Ray, who got me started in the kitchen. One day on her show, she made turkey burgers with apples, caramelized onions and Dijon mustard. I knew I had to make these burgers for the family, as we love apples and always have a plethora in our house, especially during the fall. The apple adds tons of flavor and helps keep the burgers moist. The sharp Cheddar cheese, maple syrup and Dijon mustard bring it all home to create one stellar burger!

SERVES 4

1 lb (450 g) ground turkey

1 medium Gala apple, cored and grated

½ medium yellow onion, diced

2 cloves garlic, minced

2 tbsp (30 g) Dijon mustard, divided

½ tsp poultry seasoning

1 tsp salt

½ cup (28 g) panko breadcrumbs

2 tbsp (30 ml) olive oil

4 slices sharp Cheddar cheese

1 tbsp (15 ml) pure maple syrup

4 hamburger buns

1 medium Gala apple, thinly sliced

Shredded lettuce (optional)

In a large bowl, combine the turkey, apple, onion, garlic, 1 tablespoon (15 g) of the mustard, poultry seasoning, salt and breadcrumbs. Form the mixture into 4 equal patties.

Heat the oil in a medium skillet over medium-high heat. Add the patties and cook them for 5 to 6 minutes per side, or until the patties' internal temperatures reach 165°F (74°C). During the last minute of cooking, add 1 slice of the Cheddar cheese on top of each patty and allow it to melt.

While the burgers are cooking, combine the maple syrup and remaining 1 tablespoon (15 g) of mustard in a small bowl. Set the bowl aside.

To serve, place the burgers on the hamburger buns and top them with the sliced apple, 1 tablespoon (15 ml) of the maple syrup sauce and the lettuce (if using).

Sheet Pan Italian Pepper Mini Meatloaves

Nothing screams comfort food more than meatloaf, but this isn't your mama's meatloaf. These mini meatloaves are stuffed with peppers, garlic and cheese to bring you the ultimate sheet pan dinner!

SERVES 4

8 oz (224 g) ground beef

8 oz (224 g) Italian sausage

½ medium yellow onion, diced

¼ medium red bell pepper, diced

¼ medium green bell pepper, diced

2 cloves garlic, minced

¼ cup (68 g) tomato paste

1 large egg

⅔ cup (80 g) Italian breadcrumbs

2 tbsp (22 g) shredded Parmesan cheese

1 tbsp (15 ml) Worcestershire sauce

1 tsp Italian seasoning

½ tsp salt

1 (8-oz [224-g]) block mozzarella cheese, cut into 32 cubes

¼ cup (60 ml) marinara sauce

Mashed potatoes or vegetables, for serving

Preheat the oven to 400°F (204°C). Line a 12 x 17–inch (30 x 43–cm) baking sheet with aluminum foil and spray it with cooking spray.

In a large bowl, mix together the beef, sausage, onion, red bell pepper, green bell pepper, garlic, tomato paste, egg, breadcrumbs, Parmesan cheese, Worcestershire sauce, Italian seasoning and salt.

Shape the mixture into 8 equal loaves. (If you like, you can weigh the mixture and divide by 8 to make 8 precisely equal loaves.)

Place 4 cubes of the mozzarella cheese into each meatloaf and wrap the meat around them tightly, making sure none of the cheese is exposed.

Place the meatloaves on the prepared baking sheet and spread ½ tablespoon (8 ml) of the marinara sauce on top of each meatloaf.

Bake the meatloaves in the oven for 20 to 25 minutes, or until the internal temperature of the meatloaves reaches 165°F (74°C).

Place 2 meatloaves on each plate. Serve them with mashed potatoes or the vegetable of your choice.

Poor Man's Tacos

This recipe might be my favorite in the entire book, and not only because it's essentially a deconstructed taco, but also because this recipe was my grandmother's. When my sister and I would visit her while we were growing up, she would make us these poor man's tacos and a side of freshly squeezed orange juice. (Right, Jill?!) My grandmother's version consisted of a bowl of corn chips, taco meat, shredded cheese and lettuce, but I've given it an upgrade with chorizo and black beans. I know my rendition, as well as this entire book, is something she would be proud of.

SERVES 4

POOR MAN'S TACOS

1 lb (450 g) chorizo

⅔ cup (40 g) canned black beans, drained and rinsed

1 (9¼-oz [260-g]) bag Fritos Scoops! corn chips

1 cup (120 g) shredded Cheddar cheese

1 cup (75 g) shredded lettuce

OPTIONAL TOPPINGS

Diced tomatoes

Guacamole

Sour cream

Cilantro

To make the poor man's tacos, add the chorizo to a medium skillet over medium heat, breaking it into crumbles with a wooden spoon. Cook the chorizo for 14 minutes, then add the black beans. Continue cooking for 2 to 3 minutes, until the black beans are heated through.

Place the corn chips in bowls and top them with the chorizo mixture. Top the chorizo with the Cheddar cheese, lettuce and any of the optional toppings before serving. We like to add chopped cilantro.

Cubano Skillet Calzone

Recently while dining at a pizza restaurant, I noticed they offered a Cuban pizza. All those delicious flavors on a pizza. I knew I had to make my own. While you can certainly make this a pizza, a calzone is more fun and double the crust, so no one's complaining.

SERVES 4

1 lb (450 g) frozen pizza dough, thawed

½ tsp ground cumin

½ tsp garlic powder

½ tsp dried oregano

1 tbsp (15 g) yellow mustard

1 tbsp (14 g) mayonnaise

1 cup (108 g) shredded Swiss cheese, divided

1 cup (130 g) shredded mozzarella cheese, divided

4 oz (112 g) smoked deli ham

4 oz (112 g) pastrami

12 to 16 slices dill pickle

Preheat the oven to 400°F (204°C). Grease the bottom and sides of a 10-inch (25-cm) cast-iron skillet.

Divide the pizza dough in half and, on a lightly floured surface, roll each half into a 12-inch (30-cm) circle. Place one of the circles into the prepared skillet.

In a small bowl, combine the cumin, garlic powder and oregano.

Spread the mustard all over the surface of the pizza dough in the skillet, leaving a ½-inch (13-mm) border. Repeat this process with the mayonnaise. Sprinkle the mustard-mayonnaise mixture with the cumin mixture. Top the dough in the skillet with ½ cup (54 g) of the Swiss cheese and ½ cup (65 g) of the mozzarella cheese.

Layer the ham, followed by the pastrami, on the cheeses. Top the pastrami with the remaining ½ cup (54 g) of Swiss cheese, the remaining ½ cup (65 g) of mozzarella cheese and enough dill pickles to cover the surface.

Place the remaining dough circle on top of the filling in the skillet. Pinch the edges of the bottom crust and top crust together to seal the calzone. Cut 2 small slits in the top of the dough to vent steam as the calzone bakes. Bake the calzone for 20 to 25 minutes, or until golden brown. Slice it into 8 pieces before serving.

Salsa Verde Chile Pork Enchiladas

Every Christmas my mother-in-law makes white chicken enchiladas—they were my father-in-law's favorite. I kept the same concept but switched shredded pork for the chicken, added some spice and upgraded the white sauce. It's an enchilada dish I know my father-in-law would devour!

SERVES 8

PORK ENCHILADAS

1 tsp garlic powder

1 tsp ground cumin

1 tsp chili powder

½ tsp paprika

½ tsp black pepper

¼ tsp salt

1½ lbs (675 g) pork tenderloin

Juice of 1 orange

Juice of 2 limes

½ cup (120 ml) vegetable stock or water

¾ cup (180 ml) salsa verde, divided

2 tbsp (6 g) coarsely chopped fresh cilantro

8 (8-inch [20-cm]) flour tortillas

2 cups (240 g) shredded Mexican-style cheese, divided

WHITE SAUCE

¾ cup (120 g) sour cream

1 (4-oz [112-g]) can chopped green chiles

Pico de Gallo (page 12), for garnish

Preheat the oven to 400°F (204°C).

To make the pork enchiladas, mix together the garlic powder, cumin, chili powder, paprika, black pepper and salt in a small bowl. Rub the seasoning mixture all over the pork tenderloin.

In a 2.3-quart (2.2-L) baking dish, combine the orange juice, lime juice and stock.

Place the pork tenderloin in the baking dish and roast for 20 minutes. Flip the pork, and roast for another 20 to 25 minutes, or until the pork registers 145°F (63°C) in the middle.

Remove the pork from the oven and let it cool. When it is cool enough to handle, transfer it to a cutting board, set the baking dish aside and shred the meat.

Pour ¼ cup (60 ml) of the salsa verde in the bottom of the baking dish.

Transfer the shredded pork to a large bowl and add the remaining ½ cup (120 ml) of salsa verde and cilantro. Stir to combine.

Fill each tortilla with ¼ cup (63 g) of the pork mixture and 2 tablespoons (16 g) of the cheese. Roll the tortilla around the filling, tucking in the filling as you roll. Place the tortillas seam side down in the baking dish.

To make the white sauce, combine the sour cream and green chiles in a medium bowl. Pour the sauce over the enchiladas and top them with the remaining 1 cup (120 g) of cheese.

Bake the enchiladas for 10 to 15 minutes, or until the cheese is golden and bubbly. Top the enchiladas with the pico de gallo before serving.

*See photo on page 36.

Peach and Ginger Barbecue Pulled Pork

Peach, ginger and pork go so well together. They're a triple threat in this pulled pork that we pile high on hamburger buns. It's great for a weeknight meal on large buns or to serve a crowd on slider buns.

SERVES 6

2 tbsp (18 g) paprika

1 tbsp (9 g) brown sugar

½ tbsp (4 g) black pepper

½ tbsp (5 g) chili powder

1 tsp garlic powder

½ tbsp (8 g) plus ½ tsp salt, divided

⅛ tsp cayenne pepper

2 tbsp (30 g) Dijon mustard

1 (3-lb [1.4-kg]) pork shoulder

½ cup (123 g) ketchup

2 tbsp (30 ml) apple cider vinegar

2 tsp (10 g) grated fresh ginger

1 tbsp (15 ml) Worcestershire sauce

1 (29-oz [822-g]) can sliced peaches in 100% juice, drained

6 hamburger buns or 12 slider buns

Preheat the oven to 325°F (163°C).

In a small bowl, combine the paprika, brown sugar, black pepper, chili powder, garlic powder, ½ tablespoon (8 g) of salt and cayenne pepper.

Spread the Dijon mustard all over the surface of the pork shoulder and sprinkle it with the spice mixture. Rub in the mixture well.

In a medium bowl, combine the ketchup, vinegar, ginger, Worcestershire sauce and remaining ½ teaspoon of salt.

Place the pork in a large Dutch oven. Pour the sauce over the top and add the peaches. Stir to combine and cover the Dutch oven.

Roast the pork for 3 hours, or until the pork shreds easily with a fork. Serve the pulled pork on the hamburger buns.

Deluxe Cheeseburger Sloppy Joes

Sloppy Joes give me nostalgia. Not because we ate them a lot when I was growing up, but because they make me think of a 1950s diner: girls bellying up to the counter, in their poodle skirts and cardigans, to order a sloppy Joe, along with a plate full of fries and a bubbly fountain drink with two straws. These sloppy Joes have gotten an upgrade in the form of a delicious deluxe cheeseburger that features pickles, cheese and lettuce, but I still serve them just as I imagine they did in a fifties-era soda shop.

SERVES 6

¼ cup (38 g) diced yellow onion

1 lb (450 g) ground beef

1 tsp seasoned salt, plus more as needed

½ tsp black pepper, plus more as needed

⅓ cup (48 g) dill pickle slices

3 tbsp (42 g) mayonnaise

2 tbsp (32 g) ketchup

2 tbsp (30 g) yellow mustard

1 tbsp (15 ml) Worcestershire sauce

1 tsp dried minced onion

1 tsp garlic powder

6 hamburger buns, for serving

1 cup (120 g) shredded Cheddar cheese, for serving

Shredded lettuce, for serving

In a medium skillet over medium heat, sauté the onion for about 5 minutes, or until it is soft. Add the beef, seasoned salt and black pepper and stir to combine. Cook until the meat is browned and cooked through, 7 to 10 minutes.

Stir in the pickles, mayonnaise, ketchup, mustard, Worcestershire sauce, minced onion and garlic powder. Simmer for 5 minutes. If desired, add more seasoned salt and black pepper.

To serve, place the beef mixture on the hamburger buns and top with the Cheddar cheese and lettuce.

Sheet Pan Monte Cristo Pizza

My all-time favorite sandwich is a "World Famous Monte Cristo," and I used to order it from that restaurant all the time. The restaurant is gone now, but my love for the sandwich is still strong. Therefore, I thought I'd turn it into a delicious pizza and I immediately fell in love all over again. Who doesn't love a pizza that's dusted with powdered sugar and dipped in raspberry jam?

SERVES 4

1 (14-oz [392-g]) package Wewalka Classic Pizza Dough

1 tbsp (14 g) mayonnaise

1 tbsp (15 g) Dijon mustard

12 slices deli ham

10 slices Colby Jack cheese

12 slices deli turkey

10 slices Swiss cheese

¼ cup (33 g) powdered sugar

¼ cup (81 g) red raspberry preserves

Preheat the oven to 400°F (204°C) and spray a 10 x 15–inch (25 x 38–cm) baking sheet with cooking spray.

Using your fingers, spread the pizza dough all the way to the edges of the prepared baking sheet.

Spread the mayonnaise and mustard over the dough.

Add the ham to create the first layer, the Colby Jack cheese to create the second layer, the turkey to create the third layer and the Swiss cheese to create the fourth layer.

Bake the pizza for 15 to 20 minutes, or until the crust is golden brown and crispy.

Sprinkle the pizza with the powdered sugar and serve it with the preserves.

Cajun Red Beans and Rice Stuffed Peppers

Stuffed peppers were a staple in our house when I was growing up. My mother would make classic stuffed peppers with beef, tomatoes and rice. I'll admit it was not my favorite dish, but I was a picky eater back then and green peppers were not in my food pyramid. But classic stuffed peppers get a major upgrade when red beans, flavorful rice and Cajun sausage are added to the mix. Plus, everything is cooked in one pan. It's a dish we can all go running to the table for!

SERVES 6

6 medium bell peppers (any color), tops and seeds removed

⅓ cup (80 ml) water

1 (8.8-oz [246-g]) bag ready-made Spanish rice, cooked according to package directions

1 (15-oz [420-g]) can red kidney beans, drained and rinsed

6½ oz (182 g) Cajun andouille sausage, sliced into rounds and quartered

2 medium ribs celery, coarsely chopped

1 medium yellow onion, diced

1 tbsp (15 ml) hot sauce

1 tbsp (9 g) Cajun seasoning

⅓ cup (80 ml) tomato sauce

1 tbsp (9 g) garlic powder

Preheat the oven to 350°F (177°C).

Place the bell peppers into a 2.3-quart (2.2-L) baking dish and pour in the water.

In a large bowl, combine the cooked rice, beans, sausage, celery, onion, hot sauce, Cajun seasoning, tomato sauce and garlic powder.

Place the filling in the bell peppers and bake them for 25 to 30 minutes, or until they are cooked through.

Let the bell peppers cool. When they are cool enough to handle, slice each one in half before serving.

Pork Chops with Sweet and Spicy Apple Salsa

It's no secret that apples and pork go well together. There's a whole festival dedicated to the pairing a few towns over from where I live. My husband puts applesauce on his Pork Rind Schnitzel (page 39) so it was a no-brainer to make a delicious apple salsa with the spicy flavor of jalapeño and a little sweetness from honey and mint.

SERVES 6

APPLE SALSA

2 medium Jazz or Pink Lady apples, cored and diced

1 medium jalapeño, seeded and diced

½ medium red onion, diced

½ medium red bell pepper, diced

½ tsp salt

Juice of ½ lime

1 tbsp (15 ml) honey

1 tbsp (3 g) finely chopped fresh mint

1 tbsp (3 g) finely chopped fresh cilantro

PORK CHOPS

2 tbsp (18 g) brown sugar

2 tsp (10 g) salt

1 tsp black pepper

1 tsp garlic powder

1 tsp smoked paprika

½ tsp onion powder

½ tsp ground cumin

½ tsp ground ginger

¼ tsp ground cinnamon

6 bone-in, center-cut pork chops

2 tbsp (30 ml) olive oil

To make the apple salsa, combine the apples, jalapeño, onion, bell pepper, salt, lime juice, honey, mint and cilantro in a small bowl. Place the mixture in the refrigerator.

To make the pork chops, combine the brown sugar, salt, black pepper, garlic powder, smoked paprika, onion powder, cumin, ginger and cinnamon in a medium bowl.

Sprinkle 1 teaspoon of the spice mixture over each side of the pork chops.

Heat a large cast-iron skillet over medium heat and add the oil. Sear the pork chops for 4 to 5 minutes per side, or until their internal temperature reaches 145°F (63°C).

Top the pork chops with the apple salsa before serving.

Thai Coconut Steak Tacos

I just love a good fusion, don't you? Using sweet, sour, bitter and heat to create an umami flavor profile in these tacos is a great way to pack a punch. I highly recommend you drizzle the tacos with the peanut sauce from page 31.

SERVES 4

1 ½ lbs (675 g) flank steak

½ cup (120 ml) canned coconut milk

2 tbsp (30 ml) fish sauce

2 tbsp (30 ml) fresh lime juice

2 cloves garlic, minced

2 green onions, coarsely chopped

1 tbsp (9 g) brown sugar

1 tbsp (15 g) minced fresh ginger

¼ tsp red pepper flakes (optional)

2 tbsp (30 ml) olive oil

8 (8-inch [20-cm]) flour or corn tortillas

Finely chopped green onions, for garnish

Shredded carrots, for garnish

Finely chopped fresh cilantro, for garnish

Cut the steak against the grain into ½-inch (13-mm) strips and place them in a large plastic zip-top bag.

Add the coconut milk, fish sauce, lime juice, garlic, green onions, brown sugar, ginger and red pepper flakes, if using. Let the steak marinate overnight, or at least 2 hours, in the refrigerator. Allow the steak to come to room temperature before cooking.

Heat the oil in a large skillet over medium-high heat. Carefully add the steak and cook for 4 to 5 minutes per side for medium-rare, 5 to 6 minutes for medium or 6 to 7 minutes for medium-well.

Place the steak in the tortillas and top with the finely chopped green onions, carrots and cilantro.

Smoked Sausage with Apple and Onion Kraut

This is another recipe that reminds me of my dad. Each year, when we travel to Wyoming, he always cooks brats and serves them with sauerkraut. I took his recipe for sauerkraut but swapped the cabbage for apples and onions. The results are fantastic. This apple and onion kraut is delicious on top of brats, straight from the pan or in a Reuben sandwich.

SERVES 6

4 tbsp (60 g) butter, divided

1 tbsp (15 ml) olive oil

2 medium yellow onions, thinly sliced

½ tsp salt

2 medium Fuji or Gala apples, cored and thinly sliced

2 tbsp (18 g) brown sugar

2 tbsp (30 ml) apple cider vinegar

½ tsp caraway seeds, plus more for garnish

6 fully cooked smoked sausages

6 hot dog buns, for serving

In a large skillet over medium heat, combine 3 tablespoons (45 g) of the butter and the oil. When the butter is melted, add the onions and stir to coat them. Cook the onions for about 10 minutes, or until they begin to soften. Add the salt and cook, stirring occasionally, for 10 to 15 minutes, until the onions are dark brown. If you notice the onions starting to brown too quickly, reduce the heat to medium-low.

Add the remaining 1 tablespoon (15 g) of butter, apples, brown sugar, vinegar and caraway seeds. Sauté for 5 minutes and then add the sausages.

Cook the sausages for 8 to 10 minutes, or until they are heated through. Place them in the hot dog buns and top them with the apple and onion kraut and additional caraway seeds.

COMFORT FROM
the Docks

Neither my husband nor I grew up eating seafood, but that doesn't mean we're not going to expose our children to it. Since they were table age, we've gone by the motto "You have to try at least one bite." If they decide they don't like it, fine, but they can't claim not to like it until they've actually tried it. There's nothing worse than dirtying the entire kitchen for a meal your family turns their noses up at. So, when I first served Mexican Street Corn Shrimp Pasta (page 67) and my daughter initially snubbed it, I felt defeated. But after trying it, she proceeded to devour it and then asked for a second helping, so I knew it would be a recipe to put into our rotation. The best part? There was only one pot to be cleaned.

This also happens when I serve dinner to my husband. When I made the Greek Tilapia Tacos with Tzatziki Sauce and Pickled Red Onions (page 75), I was sure he'd make a PB&J instead—the ultimate insult. Turns out he loved them! The same thing happened with the Raspberry-Chipotle Salmon with Broccoli (page 72). I taught a meal-prep class for a hot minute and this was one of the most popular dishes, but would my husband feel the same way as my students? Yes, it's a winner! The red raspberry preserves go so well with the chiles that you'll hardly notice the heat lingering in the back of your throat.

While these recipes may not be traditional, I challenge you to make these one-pan dishes and not fall in love.

Mexican Street Corn Shrimp Pasta

Street corn is by far one of the best things on Earth. But who would have thought to pair it with shrimp? This girl. Then I took it a step further and added delicious carbs in the form of pasta. I brought this dish over to my neighbor's house and her daughter told me she wanted it for her birthday for the rest of her life because she loved it so much. Comments like that are what keep me doing what I'm passionate about—feeding loved ones.

SERVES 6

2 cups (350 g) fresh or frozen corn

3 tbsp (45 ml) olive oil, divided

12 oz (336 g) frozen peeled, deveined and precooked large shrimp, thawed

1 medium jalapeño, diced

2 cloves garlic, minced

1 tsp chili powder

1 tsp salt

⅛ tsp cayenne pepper

1 tbsp (9 g) cornstarch

2 cups (480 ml) milk

1 cup (240 ml) hot water

12 oz (336 g) farfalle pasta

7 oz (196 g) Chihuahua cheese

Cotija cheese, for garnish

Coarsely chopped fresh cilantro, for garnish

Lime wedges, for garnish

Heat a large pot over medium heat. Add the corn and cook for 8 to 10 minutes, until it is charred. Transfer the corn to a plate.

Add 1 tablespoon (15 ml) of the oil to the pot, then add the shrimp in an even layer and cook them for 2 to 3 minutes per side, or until they're pink and opaque. Transfer the shrimp to the plate with the corn, and when they're cool enough to handle, remove the tails.

Add the remaining 2 tablespoons (30 ml) of oil to the pot. Add the jalapeño and garlic and cook until they are soft, 2 to 3 minutes. Add the chili powder, salt and cayenne pepper and cook for 1 minute. Then stir in the cornstarch and cook until the mixture is smooth, about 1 minute.

Whisk in the milk and water, then add the pasta. Bring the pasta to a boil. Reduce the heat to medium-low and cook for 15 minutes.

Fold in the corn, shrimp and Chihuahua cheese.

Transfer the pasta to a serving dish and top it with the Cotija cheese, cilantro and lime wedges.

Cajun Tilapia with Mango-Lime Slaw

I love pairing a little heat with something sweet, and that's how these tacos were born. The sweetness from the mango pairs beautifully with the Cajun spices on the tilapia to create a fish taco that'll earn its rightful spot on Taco Tuesday!

SERVES 4

CAJUN TILAPIA

4 (6-oz [168-g]) tilapia fillets

2 tbsp (18 g) Cajun seasoning

2 tbsp (30 ml) olive oil

MANGO-LIME SLAW

2 tbsp (30 ml) fresh lime juice

1 tbsp (15 ml) honey

1 tbsp (15 ml) apple cider vinegar

1 clove garlic, minced

½ tsp salt

¼ tsp black pepper

1 tbsp (15 ml) olive oil

1 cup (165 g) thinly sliced mango

8 (8-inch [20-cm]) tortillas

To make the Cajun tilapia, season the tilapia fillets on both sides with the Cajun seasoning.

Heat the oil in a medium skillet over medium heat. Add the tilapia and cook for 2 to 3 minutes per side, until the fish flakes easily with a fork.

To make the mango-lime slaw, whisk together the lime juice, honey, vinegar, garlic, salt, black pepper and oil in a medium bowl. Stir in the mango.

To serve, divide the tilapia among the tortillas. Top each serving with the mango-lime slaw.

Crab Rangoon Hot Dish

My sister used to work at a Chinese restaurant. When it was her shift, I'd always ask for extra crab Rangoon. I've taken the delicious sweet and crunchy appetizer and turned it into a casserole worthy of a main dish. Don't forget the crunchy wonton strips on the top for the ultimate crunch factor!

SERVES 4

2 tbsp (30 ml) olive oil

½ cup (75 g) diced yellow onion

2 cloves garlic, minced

2 tbsp (16 g) all-purpose flour

1½ cups (360 ml) vegetable stock

1½ cups (360 ml) milk

8 oz (224 g) room-temperature cream cheese

1 tsp toasted sesame oil

1 tsp Worcestershire sauce

8 oz (224 g) lump crabmeat

9 oven-ready lasagna noodles, broken into pieces

¼ cup (45 g) shredded Parmesan cheese

Wonton strips, for garnish

Finely chopped green onions, for garnish

Heat the oil in a large skillet over medium heat. Add the onion and garlic and sauté until they're translucent, about 5 minutes. Stir in the flour and cook for 1 minute.

Slowly whisk in the stock and milk. Add the cream cheese, sesame oil, Worcestershire sauce, crabmeat and lasagna noodles. Bring the mixture to a boil, then reduce the heat to medium-low, cover the skillet and cook for 15 minutes.

Stir in the Parmesan cheese. Top the hot dish with the wonton strips and green onions before serving.

Raspberry-Chipotle Salmon with Broccoli

Believe it or not, I didn't try salmon until I was thirty-four years old. Now I slather it with barbecue sauce, lemon pepper, tzatziki, you name it— but this raspberry-chipotle sauce tops the list. It's a sweet heat that pairs wonderfully with the meatiness of the salmon. When this sauced salmon is served alongside roasted broccoli, you have an entire meal cooked on one sheet pan, making for an easy cleanup. It's quickly become a healthy part of my family's weekly rotation, and it will become one of yours too.

SERVES 4

½ cup (163 g) raspberry preserves

1 tbsp (17 g) chipotles in adobo

1 clove garlic, minced

1 lb (450 g) wild-caught salmon fillets

2 to 3 cups (350 to 525 g) broccoli florets

2 tbsp (30 ml) olive oil

½ tsp garlic salt

¼ tsp black pepper

2 tbsp (22 g) grated Parmesan cheese

Preheat the oven to 450°F (232°C) and spray a 12 x 17–inch (30 x 43–cm) baking sheet with cooking spray.

In a small bowl, combine the raspberry preserves, chipotles in adobo and garlic. Spread this mixture on top of the salmon fillets and place the fillets on one side of the prepared baking sheet.

In a large bowl, toss the broccoli with the oil, garlic salt and black pepper. Place the broccoli on the opposite side of the baking sheet.

Roast the salmon and broccoli for 10 minutes. Remove the baking sheet from the oven and immediately top the broccoli with the Parmesan cheese.

Greek Tilapia Tacos with Tzatziki Sauce and Pickled Red Onions

I can't take credit for this recipe—it was the brainchild of my dad. We had a conversation about this book one day and he said, "Why don't you use those pickled onions you love so much with some tzatziki sauce and make tacos?" Sure enough, these fish tacos are fresh and fabulous!

SERVES 4

TILAPIA

4 (6-oz [168-g]) tilapia fillets

2 tsp (6 g) Greek seasoning

PICKLED RED ONIONS

1 medium red onion, thinly sliced

Juice of ½ lemon

½ tsp salt

2 tbsp (6 g) coarsely chopped fresh cilantro

TZATZIKI SAUCE

½ cup (133 g) grated cucumber

1 cup (245 g) plain Greek yogurt

2 cloves garlic, minced

1 tbsp (15 ml) fresh lemon juice

1 tbsp (3 g) coarsely chopped fresh dill

½ tsp salt

¼ tsp black pepper

8 mini naan flatbreads

To make the tilapia, preheat the oven to 400°F (204°C) and spray a 12 x 17–inch (30 x 43–cm) baking sheet with cooking spray.

Place the tilapia on the prepared baking sheet and sprinkle it with the Greek seasoning. Bake the tilapia for 10 to 12 minutes, or until the fish easily flakes with a fork.

Meanwhile, make the pickled red onions. In a medium bowl, combine the onion, lemon juice, salt and cilantro. Refrigerate the onion for at least 1 hour.

To make the tzatziki sauce, place the cucumber in a clean kitchen towel and wring it dry, squeezing out as much liquid as possible.

In a medium bowl, combine the cucumber, yogurt, garlic, lemon juice, dill, salt and black pepper.

Flake the tilapia; then place about 2 tablespoons (30 g) of the fish onto each mini naan flatbread. Top each taco with 1 tablespoon (15 g) of tzatziki sauce and 1 tablespoon (8 g) of pickled red onions before serving.

Barbecue Shrimp with White Cheddar Grits

This dish is inspired by a local café where I had grits with white Cheddar and perfectly cooked shrimp. That bowl was out of this world. This is my take on the dish, which turned out just as amazing! Sometimes I put an egg on the grits and serve this dish for breakfast.

SERVES 4

WHITE CHEDDAR GRITS

2 cups (480 ml) milk

2 cups (480 ml) water

1½ tsp (8 g) salt

1 cup (170 g) stone-ground white grits

2 tbsp (30 ml) heavy cream

2 tbsp (30 g) butter

½ cup (60 g) grated sharp white Cheddar cheese

¼ tsp black pepper

6 slices bacon

BLACKENED SHRIMP

2 tbsp (18 g) paprika

1 tbsp (9 g) brown sugar

½ tbsp (4 g) black pepper

½ tbsp (5 g) chili powder

1 tsp garlic powder

1 tsp onion powder

½ tbsp (8 g) salt

⅛ tsp cayenne pepper

12 oz (336 g) frozen extra-large shrimp, peeled and deveined

1 tbsp (15 ml) olive oil

1 tbsp (15 g) butter

¼ cup (13 g) finely chopped green onions

To make the white Cheddar grits, combine the milk and water in a medium skillet over medium-high heat. Bring the mixture to a boil. Stir in the salt and grits and reduce the heat to low. Cook the grits for 10 minutes. Add the cream and butter, cover the skillet, and cook until the grits are smooth and creamy, about 40 minutes. Take the grits off the heat and stir in the Cheddar cheese and black pepper. Place the grits in a large bowl and cover it to keep them warm.

Return the skillet to medium-high heat. Add the bacon and cook it on both sides until it is brown and crispy, about 5 minutes total. Transfer the bacon to a paper towel to drain, then crumble it. Drain the skillet.

To make the blackened shrimp, combine the paprika, brown sugar, black pepper, chili powder, garlic powder, onion powder, salt and cayenne pepper in a small bowl. Sprinkle the shrimp with the seasoning mix.

Heat the skillet over medium heat. Add the oil and butter and allow the butter to melt. Add the shrimp in an even layer and cook for 2 to 3 minutes per side, or until the shrimp are pink and opaque. Transfer the shrimp to a plate to cool. Once they're cool enough to handle, remove their tails.

Divide the grits among 4 bowls and top each serving with the barbecue shrimp, bacon and green onions.

Tuna Pot Pie Biscuit Casserole

I have always loved tuna. Tuna casserole was always a family favorite when I was a little girl—and it still is—but how about removing the noodles and topping the whole thing with a crescent roll? You see, I'm not a fan of pie crust, but I can get down with a flaky crescent roll!

SERVES 4

¼ cup (60 g) butter

½ cup (75 g) diced onion

2 cups (300 g) frozen mixed vegetables

½ cup (60 g) all-purpose flour

1 tbsp (15 g) Dijon mustard

¾ tsp salt

½ tsp black pepper

1¼ cups (300 ml) milk

1 cup (240 ml) vegetable stock

3 (5-oz [140-g]) cans tuna packed in water, drained

1 cup (120 g) shredded Cheddar cheese

1 (8-oz [224-g]) can crescent dough sheet or crescent roll dough, perforations pressed together

Preheat the oven to 350°F (177°C).

Melt the butter in a large oven-safe skillet over medium heat. Add the onion and mixed vegetables and sauté for 5 minutes, or until the onion is translucent. Whisk in the flour, mustard, salt and black pepper.

Slowly whisk in the milk and vegetable stock. Bring the mixture to a boil, then reduce the heat to medium-low. Add the tuna and cook for 5 minutes. Sprinkle the Cheddar cheese on top.

Unroll the crescent dough and place it over the filling. Cut two small slits in the top of the dough to vent any steam during baking. Bake the casserole for 18 to 20 minutes, or until the crust is golden brown. Let the casserole cool slightly before serving.

Spicy Barbecue Salmon Bowls

Sometimes the simplest things make the most delicious dinner. I'm not above using store-bought shortcuts such as barbecue sauce and frozen zucchini noodles. They help make for a healthy and quick ten-minute dinner the entire family will enjoy. The slightly spicy barbecue sauce paired with sweet mango and creamy avocado is a fantastic combination. Feel free to use a mild barbecue sauce if you're not into spiciness.

SERVES 4

1 lb (450 g) wild-caught salmon fillets

¼ cup (60 ml) sweet and spicy barbecue sauce

1 medium mango, diced

1 medium avocado, diced

Juice of ½ lime

2 (12-oz [336-g]) packages zucchini noodles, cooked

Coarsely chopped fresh cilantro, for garnish

Preheat the oven to 450°F (232°C) and spray a 12 x 17–inch (30 x 43–cm) baking sheet with cooking spray.

Place the salmon fillets on the baking sheet and spread the barbecue sauce evenly over each one. Bake them for 10 minutes, or until the sauce is slightly caramelized and a fork can easily be inserted into the fillets.

In the meantime, combine the mango, avocado and lime juice in a medium bowl.

Evenly distribute the zucchini noodles among 4 bowls. Top the noodles with the salmon and mango-avocado salsa and cilantro before serving.

Tzatziki Stuffed Salmon Cakes

Salmon and dill were made for each other, so when I was deciding what
kind of seafood cakes to make, I knew I had to use this pair. The meatiness
of the salmon marries perfectly with the pungency of the herbs
to produce a light and fresh salmon cake.

SERVES 4

SALMON CAKES

1 (14¾-oz [413-g]) can
boneless, skinless salmon
in water, drained

1 cup (120 g)
breadcrumbs

2 large eggs, beaten

½ cup (75 g) shredded
cucumber, packed

2 cloves garlic, minced

1 tbsp (15 ml) fresh
lemon juice

2 tbsp (6 g) coarsely
chopped fresh dill

1 tbsp (3 g) coarsely
chopped fresh mint

1 tsp salt

¼ cup (60 ml) olive oil

OPTIONAL
PAIRINGS

Arugula or spinach

Tzatziki Sauce (page 75)

Feta cheese

Pickled Red Onions
(page 75)

Lemon wedges

To make the salmon cakes, combine the salmon,
breadcrumbs, eggs, cucumber, garlic, lemon juice,
dill, mint and salt in a large bowl. Mix well.

Using your hands, form the mixture into 8 (3-inch
[8-cm]) patties.

Heat the oil in a large skillet over medium heat.

Add the salmon cakes to the skillet in batches,
being careful not to crowd the pan. Cook for
3 to 4 minutes per side, or until they are light
golden brown.

Serve the salmon cakes over a bed of arugula, or
topped with a little Tzatziki Sauce, feta cheese and
Pickled Red Onions.

General Tso's Shrimp Po'boy

Whenever my family orders Chinese food, we always order General Tso's chicken. The flavorful, sweet and slightly spicy sauce is our favorite. When I make this recipe, I pan-sear the shrimp in the sauce instead of frying them. This method makes for a lighter take-out dish that's super fun to make at home.

SERVES 4

SRIRACHA MAYONNAISE

¼ cup (56 g) mayonnaise

2 tbsp (30 ml) Sriracha

GENERAL TSO'S SHRIMP

1 lb (450 g) large cooked shrimp, peeled, deveined and tails removed

2 tbsp (18 g) cornstarch

2 cloves garlic, minced

1 tsp minced fresh ginger

¼ cup (60 ml) soy sauce

1 tbsp (15 ml) rice wine vinegar

2 tbsp (30 ml) hoisin sauce

2 tbsp (18 g) brown sugar

¼ tsp red pepper flakes (optional)

2 tbsp (30 ml) toasted sesame oil

4 French sandwich rolls

Coleslaw or thinly sliced cabbage, for garnish

To make the Sriracha mayonnaise, stir together the mayonnaise and Sriracha in a small bowl. Set the Sriracha mayonnaise aside.

To make the General Tso's shrimp, toss together the shrimp and cornstarch in a large bowl.

In a medium bowl, whisk together the garlic, ginger, soy sauce, rice wine vinegar, hoisin sauce, brown sugar and red pepper flakes, if using. Pour the sauce over the shrimp and toss to combine.

Heat the oil in a large skillet over medium-high heat. Add the shrimp and sauce and cook for 3 to 5 minutes, or until the shrimp are caramelized in the sauce.

To serve, place the cooked shrimp into the sandwich rolls and top the shrimp with the coleslaw and Sriracha mayonnaise.

CLEVER ONE-DISH
Pastabilities

Pasta, oh pasta, how we love thee. When I was growing up, we had spaghetti at least once a week and it was my favorite. My mom's spaghetti sauce is crazy good and we always served the meal with a garden salad (blue cheese dressing for me, please). In our home these days, it's no different. We serve pasta at least once a week and a frequent request from my son is the Deluxe Pizza Spaghetti (page 94)—don't forget the garlic bread.

Now if my husband is picking dinner, you better believe I'm dishing up Chili Mac Tortilla Pie (page 93). It's his favorite recipe from this book.

With these dishes, you don't have to worry about boiling the pasta in one pot and cooking the other components in another. This is a one-pot cookbook, remember? I've got you covered—just like my Philly Cheesesteak Stuffed Shells (page 106) are covered in provolone cheese sauce!

Dad's Mostaccioli

This is my dad's recipe—sort of. He makes his in a casserole dish and uses ten times more cheese than I do (if you can believe that) and a homemade pasta sauce. But to keep this one-pan friendly, I use a store-bought shortcut with jarred pasta sauce. This is one of my favorite recipes. It's a warm blanket of comforting carbs.

SERVES 6

8 oz (224 g) chorizo

8 oz (224 g) ground beef

8 oz (224 g) Italian sausage

1 tbsp (15 g) butter

1 tbsp (15 ml) olive oil

1 medium yellow onion, diced

3 cloves garlic, minced

24 oz (720 ml) marinara sauce

2 cups (480 ml) water

12 oz (336 g) mostaccioli or penne rigate pasta

½ cup (65 g) shredded mozzarella cheese

½ cup (90 g) shredded Parmesan cheese

½ cup (90 g) shredded Asiago cheese

½ cup (54 g) shredded Gruyère cheese

2 tbsp (6 g) coarsely chopped fresh parsley, for garnish

In a large skillet over medium heat, combine the chorizo, beef and Italian sausage. Cook until the meats are brown, 8 to 10 minutes. Transfer the meats to a plate.

Add the butter and oil to the skillet. Allow the butter to melt, then add the onion and garlic. Sauté for 5 minutes, or until the onion is translucent.

Stir in the marinara sauce, water and pasta. Bring the mixture to a boil, then reduce the heat to medium-low and cook for 15 minutes, or until the pasta is cooked.

Return the meats to the skillet. Add the mozzarella, Parmesan, Asiago and Gruyère cheeses. Stir to combine all the ingredients and cook until the cheeses are melted, 2 to 3 minutes. Garnish the pasta with the parsley before serving.

Black and Blue Pasta

This recipe is all mine and by that, I mean my family will not touch it. They aren't fans of mushrooms or blue cheese, but they don't know what they're missing. Their loss—I'll invite my dad and sister over and it'll be gone in no time. This pasta is a combination of a black and blue burger piled high with mushrooms, bacon and blue cheese. It's enough to send me into a carb coma, and I'm here for it!

SERVES 6

6 slices bacon

2 tbsp (30 g) butter, divided

1 lb (450 g) ribeye steak, thinly sliced

1 tbsp (15 ml) olive oil

2 cloves garlic, minced

1 medium yellow onion, coarsely chopped

8 oz (224 g) cremini mushrooms, thickly sliced

½ tsp salt

½ tsp black pepper

½ tsp dried thyme

4 cups (960 ml) beef stock

1 lb (450 g) cavatappi pasta

½ cup (60 g) sour cream

4 oz (112 g) crumbled blue cheese

2 tbsp (6 g) coarsely chopped fresh parsley

Heat a large skillet over medium heat. Add the bacon and cook until it's brown and crispy, about 5 minutes. Transfer the bacon to paper towels to drain. Do not drain the bacon fat from the skillet.

Add 1 tablespoon (15 g) of the butter to the skillet and allow the butter to melt. Add the steak to the skillet and cook for 1 to 2 minutes per side, or until it is slightly browned. Transfer it to a plate to rest.

Add the remaining 1 tablespoon (15 g) of butter and oil to the skillet. Add the garlic, onion and mushrooms and sauté them until they're soft, about 5 minutes. Season the mixture with the salt, black pepper and thyme.

Pour in the stock and pasta. Cover the skillet and bring the mixture to a boil. Reduce the heat to medium-low and simmer for 13 to 15 minutes, or until the liquid is absorbed.

Return the steak back to the skillet and stir in the sour cream. Remove the skillet from the heat. Crumble the cooled bacon.

To serve, transfer the pasta to a large serving bowl and top it with the blue cheese, bacon and parsley.

Chili Mac Tortilla Pie

This is my husband's favorite recipe in the book—I didn't even have to ask for his opinion as he was piling his second helping onto his plate and packing leftovers for the next day. There's nostalgia in a big old bowl of chili mac that instantly sends most of us back to our childhoods. It was a simple and quick dinner families could throw together without dirtying the entire kitchen. I keep the classic flavors you love, but I top it with sliced tortillas and extra cheese, because that's how we roll.

SERVES 6

1 tbsp (15 ml) olive oil

1 medium yellow onion, diced

2 cloves garlic, minced

1 tbsp (17 g) tomato paste

2 tbsp (18 g) chili powder

2 tsp (6 g) ground cumin

1½ tsp (8 g) salt

1 tsp black pepper

1 (8-oz [240-ml]) can tomato sauce

1 (15½-oz [434-g]) can kidney beans, drained and rinsed

2 cups (480 ml) beef stock

10 oz (280 g) elbow macaroni pasta

1 cup (120 g) shredded sharp Cheddar cheese, divided

2 (10-inch [25-cm]) tortillas, each cut into 6 strips

Preheat the oven to 400°F (204°C).

Heat the oil in a large cast-iron skillet over medium heat. Add the onion and garlic and cook them for 5 minutes, or until they are soft.

Stir in the tomato paste, chili powder, cumin, salt and black pepper and cook for 1 to 2 minutes.

Add the tomato sauce, beans, stock and pasta. Bring the mixture to a boil. Reduce the heat to medium-low and cook for 13 to 15 minutes, until the pasta is cooked.

Stir in ½ cup (60 g) of the Cheddar cheese. Top the pasta with the tortilla strips and remaining ½ cup (60 g) of Cheddar cheese.

Bake the pie for 20 to 25 minutes, or until the top is golden brown. Let the pie cool slightly before serving.

Deluxe Pizza Spaghetti

Like most households, pizza night is a favorite around here—but as with most meals, I like to switch things up a bit. As my husband says, "You can't ever leave anything alone." Therefore, I took one of our family's favorite varieties of pizza and turned it into a pasta. Feel free to add your favorite toppings such as mushrooms, black olives or pineapple—no one is judging you! We serve this pasta alongside a salad, some garlic bread and shakers of Parmesan cheese and red pepper flakes, and pretend we're at a local pizzeria.

SERVES 6

8 oz (224 g) Italian sausage

1 tbsp (15 ml) olive oil

2 cloves garlic, minced

1 medium yellow onion, diced

1 medium green bell pepper, diced

½ tbsp (5 g) Italian seasoning

1 tsp salt

1 (28-oz [784-g]) can petite diced tomatoes, undrained

1 cup (240 ml) water

8 oz (224 g) spaghetti

3 oz (84 g) pepperoni, coarsely chopped

¼ cup (45 g) shredded Parmesan cheese

½ cup (65 g) shredded mozzarella cheese

Sliced black olives, for garnish (optional)

Heat a large skillet over medium heat. Add the sausage and cook for 10 to 12 minutes. Transfer the sausage to a plate.

Add the oil, garlic, onion and green bell pepper to the skillet and sauté for 5 minutes. Add the Italian seasoning and salt. Stir to combine.

Add the tomatoes, water and spaghetti and bring the mixture to a boil. Reduce the heat to medium-low and cook for 13 to 15 minutes, or until the spaghetti is cooked.

Stir in the pepperoni, Parmesan cheese and mozzarella cheese before serving. Garnish the spaghetti with the black olives, if using.

Goat Cheese Macaroni and Cheese

This might be my favorite recipe in the entire book. I know that goat cheese isn't for everyone, but before you tell me you don't like it, you've got to try this pasta. The goat cheese makes for a tangy, creamy sauce that brings together the roasted red pepper and spinach so beautifully.

SERVES 6

2 tbsp (30 g) butter

2 cloves garlic, minced

¼ cup (30 g) all-purpose flour

½ tsp salt

¼ tsp black pepper

2 cups (480 ml) milk

1 cup (120 g) shredded white Cheddar cheese

4 oz (112 g) garlic and herb goat cheese

¼ cup (45 g) shredded Parmesan cheese

¼ cup (35 g) coarsely chopped roasted red bell peppers

12 oz (336 g) elbow macaroni pasta

½ cup (15 g) baby spinach

Melt the butter in a large skillet over medium heat. Add the garlic and cook for 1 minute, or until the garlic is fragrant. Stir in the flour and cook for 1 minute. Season the flour with the salt and black pepper. Whisk in the milk.

Stir in the Cheddar cheese, goat cheese, Parmesan cheese, bell peppers, pasta and spinach. Bring the mixture to a boil. Reduce the heat to medium-low and cook for 10 to 12 minutes, or until the pasta is cooked. Let the pasta cool slightly before serving.

Chicken-Bacon-Ranch Carbonara

I'll admit, I'd never had carbonara until I made this recipe. I've heard Rachael Ray talk about it for years because it's her husband's favorite dish, but I didn't know what all the fuss was about. An egg in pasta? Pssh, big deal, right? But it is a big deal. The egg coats the noodles and makes for a rich and luscious sauce you aren't going to get any other way. Don't knock it until you try it.

SERVES 6

3 tbsp (45 ml) olive oil, divided

6 slices bacon, coarsely chopped

1½ lbs (675 g) boneless, skinless chicken breasts, diced

2 tbsp (18 g) ranch seasoning

2 cups (480 ml) chicken stock

1 (8.8-oz [246-g]) box fettucine pasta

2 large egg yolks, beaten

½ cup (90 g) shredded Parmigiano-Reggiano cheese

½ tsp black pepper

Coarsely chopped fresh parsley, for garnish (optional)

Heat 2 tablespoons (30 ml) of the oil in a large skillet over medium heat. Add the bacon and cook until the bacon is brown and crispy, about 5 minutes. Transfer the bacon to a plate lined with paper towels. Do not drain the skillet. When the bacon is cool enough to handle, crumble it.

Add the remaining 1 tablespoon (15 ml) of oil to the bacon grease in the skillet. Add the chicken and cook until it's no longer pink in the center, 8 to 10 minutes. Sprinkle the chicken with the ranch seasoning.

Add the stock and pasta. Bring the mixture to a boil. Reduce the heat to medium-low and cook for 8 minutes, or until the pasta is cooked.

Pour in the egg yolks and stir so they coat the pasta. To serve, sprinkle the pasta with the crumbled bacon, Parmigiano-Reggiano cheese and black pepper, tossing to combine. Garnish with parsley, if using.

Bloody Mary Chicken Pasta

This dish is your favorite brunch drink turned into a flavorful pasta! It has everything the ultimate Bloody Mary bar would feature, like tangy horseradish, salty green olives and hot sauce, all cooked in one delicious pasta pan.

SERVES 6

1 lb (450 g) boneless, skinless chicken breasts, diced

½ tsp salt

¼ tsp black pepper

2 tbsp (30 ml) olive oil, divided

½ cup (75 g) diced onion

4 slices bacon, diced

½ cup (50 g) thinly sliced celery

2 cloves garlic, minced

1 (15-oz [420-g]) can no-sodium diced tomatoes

2½ cups (600 ml) Zing Zang Bloody Mary mix

1 tbsp (15 ml) Worcestershire sauce

1 tbsp (15 ml) hot sauce, or more to taste

2 tbsp (30 g) prepared horseradish

1 tsp sugar

½ tsp celery salt

12 oz (336 g) penne pasta

1 tbsp (15 ml) fresh lemon juice

⅔ cup (90 g) green olives, thinly sliced, for garnish

Season the chicken with the salt and black pepper. Heat 1 tablespoon (15 ml) of the oil in a large skillet over medium-high heat. Add the chicken, onion and bacon and cook until the chicken is no longer pink in the center, 8 to 10 minutes. Transfer the mixture to a plate.

Reduce the heat to medium. Add the remaining 1 tablespoon (15 ml) of oil, the celery and garlic and sauté for 3 minutes.

Add the tomatoes, Bloody Mary mix, Worcestershire sauce, hot sauce, horseradish, sugar, celery salt and pasta. Stir the chicken, onion and bacon back into the skillet. Bring the mixture to a boil, reduce the heat to medium-low and cook until the pasta is al dente, 10 to 12 minutes.

Stir the lemon juice into the pasta. Garnish the pasta with the olives before serving.

Hawaiian Macaroni and Cheese

Creamy macaroni and cheese is whisked away to the Islands by adding sweet pineapple and diced ham. It's the best of both worlds in a sweet and savory pot of melty, gooey cheeses and pasta!

SERVES 6

1 lb (450 g) orecchiette pasta, elbow macaroni pasta or small shell pasta

4 cups (960 ml) whole milk

8 oz (224 g) sharp Cheddar cheese, shredded

4 oz (112 g) Swiss cheese, shredded

2 tbsp (30 g) cream cheese

2 tbsp (30 g) butter

1 tbsp (15 g) Dijon mustard

1 tsp garlic powder

½ tsp salt

½ tsp ground ginger

⅛ tsp ground nutmeg

⅛ tsp ground turmeric

⅛ tsp cayenne pepper

1 (20-oz [560-g]) can pineapple tidbits in 100% juice, drained

8 oz (224 g) diced ham

Thinly sliced green onions, for garnish

Combine the pasta and milk in a large pot over medium heat.

Bring the milk to a simmer and cook until the pasta is tender, 8 to 10 minutes.

Remove the pasta. Stir in the Cheddar cheese, Swiss cheese, cream cheese, butter, mustard, garlic powder, salt, ginger, nutmeg, turmeric and cayenne pepper.

Fold in the pasta, pineapple and ham. Garnish the macaroni and cheese with the green onions before serving.

Mexican Chorizo Stroganoff

Instead of using thin slices of beef in this stroganoff, I opted for chorizo, mostly because my dad puts chorizo in anything he can and it always reminds me of him. Chorizo has a great mixture of aromatic flavors that makes everything taste better. I left out the mushrooms in this stroganoff because I am the only one in my family who likes them, but if you like mushrooms, add 1 cup (66 g) of thinly sliced mushrooms when you sauté the garlic.

SERVES 6

12 oz (336 g) chorizo

½ cup (75 g) diced onion

2 cloves garlic, minced

1 (10-oz [280-g]) can tomatoes with green chiles

1 cup (165 g) frozen corn

1 (10-oz [280-ml]) can red enchilada sauce

1 tsp ground cumin

2 tbsp (18 g) cornstarch

8 oz (224 g) egg noodles

½ cup (60 g) sour cream

1 cup (120 g) shredded Cheddar cheese

2 tbsp (6 g) coarsely chopped fresh cilantro, for garnish

Heat a large skillet over medium-high heat. Add the chorizo and cook until it is brown, about 7 minutes.

Add the onion and garlic and cook for 5 minutes, or until the onion is soft.

Stir in the tomatoes, corn, enchilada sauce, cumin, cornstarch and egg noodles. Bring the mixture to a boil. Reduce the heat to medium-low and cook for 6 to 7 minutes, until the pasta is cooked.

Stir in the sour cream and Cheddar cheese. Garnish the noodles with the cilantro before serving.

Philly Cheesesteak Stuffed Shells

No one's going to miss the bread in this dish! Delicious beef, onions, green peppers and cheese all stuffed into a jumbo pasta shell and covered with provolone cheese? Oh yes, I did. And that cheese sauce? Feel free to use that on nachos, as a dipping sauce or as the base of a Philly cheesesteak pizza.

SERVES 4

STUFFED SHELLS

1 tbsp (15 ml) olive oil

1 tbsp (15 g) butter

2 cloves garlic, minced

1 medium green bell pepper, diced

1 medium yellow onion, diced

8 oz (224 g) ground sirloin

1 tsp salt

½ tsp black pepper

¾ cup (92 g) ricotta cheese

⅔ cup (87 g) shredded Italian five-cheese blend

2 tbsp (30 ml) Worcestershire sauce

12 to 16 jumbo pasta shells

PROVOLONE CHEESE SAUCE

2 tbsp (30 ml) olive oil

2 tbsp (30 g) butter

2 cloves garlic, minced

2 tbsp (16 g) all-purpose flour

2 cups (480 ml) warm milk

8 oz (224 g) provolone cheese, thinly sliced or grated

1 tsp salt

½ tsp black pepper

To make the stuffed shells, combine the oil and butter in a large oven-safe skillet over medium heat. Allow the butter to melt for 1 to 2 minutes. Stir in the garlic, bell pepper, onion, sirloin, salt and black pepper. Cook until the sirloin is brown, 8 to 10 minutes. Transfer the filling to a large bowl and allow it to cool.

Once the sirloin mixture is cool, add the ricotta cheese, Italian five-cheese blend and Worcestershire sauce and mix to combine. Place the cheese mixture in a large zip-top bag and snip off one corner. Pipe the mixture into the pasta shells and set the shells aside.

Preheat the oven to 350°F (177°C).

To make the provolone cheese sauce, combine the oil and butter in the same skillet over medium heat and allow the butter to melt, about 1 to 2 minutes. Add the garlic and sauté for 1 minute. Stir in the flour and cook for 1 minute. Whisk in the milk and cook for 2 to 3 minutes. Reduce the heat to medium-low and stir in the provolone cheese, salt and black pepper.

Place the stuffed shells in the provolone cheese sauce, being careful not to overcrowd them as they need to be submerged in the sauce to cook properly. Cover the skillet and bake the stuffed shells for 30 to 35 minutes, or until the pasta is cooked. Let the shells cool slightly before serving.

Spinach-Artichoke and Ham Lasagna

If spinach-artichoke dip is on the menu, I'm ordering it. If it's at a party, you'll find me hovering over the bowl. There's something about that ooey-gooey cheese dip that makes my heart skip a beat and my tummy instantly rumble. So how about making that delicious dip, adding salty ham and sandwiching it between lasagna noodles? Makes my heart go pitter-patter just thinking about it.

SERVES 8

8 oz (224 g) ricotta cheese

8 oz (224 g) room-temperature cream cheese

1 (13¾-oz [385-g]) can quartered artichoke hearts in water, drained and coarsely chopped

10 oz (280 g) frozen spinach, thawed

1 tsp garlic powder

¾ tsp onion powder

¾ tsp salt

½ tsp black pepper

⅛ tsp ground nutmeg

1 tbsp (15 ml) milk

1 lb (450 g) cubed ham

½ cup (120 ml) water

9 oven-ready lasagna noodles

8 oz (224 g) shredded Italian five-cheese blend, divided

Preheat the oven to 350°F (177°C).

In a large bowl, combine the ricotta cheese, cream cheese, artichoke hearts, spinach, garlic powder, onion powder, salt, black pepper, nutmeg, milk and ham.

Pour the water into a 3.6-quart (3.5-L) baking dish. Lay 3 lasagna noodles in the bottom of the baking dish. Top the noodles with one-third of the spinach-artichoke mixture and ⅔ cup (87 g) of the Italian five-cheese blend. Place 3 more lasagna noodles on top of the cheese, then top the noodles with one-third of the spinach-artichoke mixture and ⅔ cup (87 g) of the Italian five-cheese blend. Repeat this process to create the last layer of the lasagna.

Cover the baking dish with foil and bake the lasagna for 30 minutes. Remove the foil and bake for 10 to 12 minutes, or until the top of the lasagna is brown. Allow the lasagna to cool for 15 minutes before slicing.

Tortellini Primavera

My family's favorite pasta is tortellini, but topping it with spaghetti sauce time after time can get boring. So I like to change it up a bit and toss the tortellini with fresh vegetables and light cheese. This tortellini primavera can be served warm or cold and makes a great potluck dish.

SERVES 6

2 tbsp (30 ml) olive oil

2 tbsp (30 g) butter

3 cloves garlic, minced

1 medium red onion, thinly sliced

1 small zucchini, sliced into semicircles

1 small yellow squash, sliced into semicircles

8 oz (224 g) cherry tomatoes

2 medium carrots, peeled and chopped into thick matchsticks

1 medium green bell pepper, thinly sliced

1 tsp Italian seasoning

½ tsp salt

¼ tsp black pepper

1 cup (240 ml) chicken stock

1 lb (450 g) frozen cheese tortellini

½ cup (90 g) shaved Parmesan cheese, divided

Juice of ½ lemon

In a large skillet over medium heat, combine the oil and butter and allow the butter to melt.

Add the garlic and cook for 1 minute. Add the onion, zucchini, squash, tomatoes, carrots and bell pepper. Sauté for 7 to 8 minutes, or until the vegetables are tender. Season them with the Italian seasoning, salt and black pepper.

Add the stock and tortellini. Cover the skillet and simmer for 5 to 6 minutes, or until the tortellini is cooked through.

Stir in ¼ cup (45 g) of the Parmesan cheese and the lemon juice.

Top the pasta with the remaining ¼ cup (45 g) of Parmesan cheese before serving.

NO-FUSS

Soups

Soups are like a warm blanket. They comfort us when we're sick, make us feel cozy when the weather outside looks scary (hello, Midwestern January) and fill our hearts with joy when we're missing someone and need a little comfort.

For my family, Sundays mean football and football means chili, so we whip up a batch of Beefy Peanut Butter Chili (page 130). You can do the same to wow your friends and cheer on your favorite team at the same time.

Know a friend who isn't feeling well and could use a little pick-me-up? I suggest Chicken Noodle Pho (page 137) to soothe what ails them.

Want to feel like a kid again with a big bowl of tomato soup and a grilled cheese sandwich? The grown-up Tomato-Pumpkin Soup with Pesto (page 123) will satisfy your nostalgia and your belly.

I love the way food has the ability to bring us all together, like a lingering hug—and that is just what this chapter is about. Bring the people in your life together over one big pot of delicious soup.

Loaded Sausage and Pierogi Soup

This soup has been on repeat since I made it the first time and just happens to be the first recipe I tested for this book, so my family has eaten it many times since. It's everything you love about a loaded potato soup but with mini pierogi, which make this soup that much better. I cannot wait for a chilly fall night, so I can put a football game on the TV and cozy up on the couch with this lovely bowl of soup that takes no time at all to prepare!

SERVES 6

8 slices bacon

1 (14-oz [392-g]) package smoked sausage, sliced into ½-inch (13-mm) rounds

2 tbsp (30 g) butter

2 cloves garlic, minced

⅓ cup (50 g) diced yellow onion

½ tsp salt

¼ tsp black pepper

3 tbsp (24 g) all-purpose flour

2 cups (480 ml) milk

2 cups (480 ml) beef stock

1 (12.8-oz [358-g]) package mini pierogi

½ cup (60 g) sour cream

Shredded Cheddar cheese, for garnish (optional)

Thinly sliced green onions, for garnish (optional)

Heat a large skillet over medium heat. Add the bacon and cook until it's brown and crispy, about 5 minutes. Transfer the bacon to a plate lined with paper towels to drain. When it's cool enough to handle, crumble the bacon.

Add the sausage to the skillet and brown it on both sides, about 5 minutes total. Transfer the sausage to the plate with the bacon.

Add the butter to the skillet, then add the garlic and onion. Sauté until the garlic and onion are soft, about 5 minutes. Season with the salt and black pepper.

Stir in the flour and cook for 1 minute. Slowly whisk in the milk and stock. Bring the mixture to a boil, and add the pierogi, sausage and half of the crumbled bacon. Reduce the heat to medium-low and cook for 10 minutes.

Remove the skillet from the heat and stir in the sour cream. Before serving, top the soup with the remaining bacon, Cheddar cheese, if using, and green onions, if using.

Supreme Nacho Soup

Chips are my weakness, especially when they are topped with cheese sauce, black beans, tomatoes, sour cream and all the fixins. This supreme nacho soup never fails. I took the classic flavors of supreme nachos, put them into a soup and then topped the soup with tortilla chips. I'll take my nachos any way I can get them! I made this recipe vegetarian-friendly, but feel free to add ground beef, chorizo or shredded chicken.

SERVES 4

2 tbsp (30 ml) olive oil, divided

1 cup (165 g) frozen corn

1 medium yellow onion, diced

1 medium jalapeño, seeded and diced

2 cloves garlic, minced

1 tsp chili powder

1 tsp ground cumin

½ tsp salt

1 (15-oz [420-g]) can black beans, drained and rinsed

1 (15-oz [420-g]) can fire-roasted tomatoes, with liquid

1 (15-oz [425-ml]) can nacho Cheddar cheese sauce

1 cup (240 ml) vegetable stock

1 cup (130 g) shredded pepper Jack cheese

½ cup (60 g) sour cream

Tortilla chips, for garnish

Finely chopped fresh cilantro, for garnish

Thinly sliced green onions, for garnish

Heat the oil in a medium Dutch oven over medium heat. Add the corn, onion, jalapeño and garlic. Sauté for 5 to 7 minutes, or until the vegetables are soft. Season the vegetables with the chili powder, cumin and salt.

Stir in the black beans, tomatoes and Cheddar cheese sauce.

Pour in the stock. Bring the mixture to a boil, reduce the heat to medium-low and simmer for 5 minutes.

Remove the soup from the heat and stir in the pepper Jack cheese and sour cream.

Serve the soup garnished with the tortilla chips, cilantro and green onions.

French Onion Blue Cheese Soup

French onion soup is at the top of my list when it comes to cold and flu season. There's something about those pieces of bread sprinkled with cheese that sends my cold into oblivion. Don't be stingy with the blue cheese. The sharp, creamy cheese blends beautifully with the sweet, deep flavors of the onions and the beefy broth.

SERVES 4

2 tbsp (30 g) butter

2 tbsp (30 ml) olive oil

8 cups (1 kg) thinly sliced Vidalia onions

2 tsp (10 g) salt, divided

1 tbsp (12 g) sugar

⅔ cup (160 ml) dry white wine

2 tbsp (16 g) all-purpose flour

1 tbsp (15 ml) Worcestershire sauce

5 cups (1.2 L) beef stock

½ tsp black pepper

4 sprigs fresh thyme

2 dried bay leaves

8 slices French bread

4 oz (112 g) blue cheese

Heat the butter and oil in a 5-quart (4.8-L) pot over medium heat. Add the onions and toss them in the mixture to coat them evenly. Cook the onions for 25 to 30 minutes, until they are soft. Reduce the heat to medium-low, add 1 teaspoon of the salt and the sugar, and cook the onions until they begin to brown, 10 to 15 minutes.

Add the wine to deglaze the pot, scraping up any brown bits with a wooden spoon. Sprinkle the flour over the mixture, stir and cook for 1 minute. Add the Worcestershire sauce, stock, remaining 1 teaspoon of salt, black pepper, thyme and bay leaves. Increase the heat to medium and bring the soup to a boil. Reduce the heat to medium-low and simmer for 30 minutes. Remove the bay leaves.

Preheat the oven broiler shortly before the soup is done simmering. Ladle the soup into oven-safe soup bowls and top each serving with 2 slices of the French bread. Top the French bread with the blue cheese and broil the cheese for about 2 minutes to melt it.

Alternatively, you can line a medium baking sheet with the slices of French bread, then sprinkle them with the blue cheese and broil them until the cheese melts, 2 to 3 minutes.

Chipotle Beef Stew

Yes, I have two beef stews in one book, but hear me out. They're totally different from each other. This one will make you feel like you're south of the border with a spicy, smoky broth, whereas the other one (page 124) is rich and hearty with fluffy dumplings. They both deserve their rightful spot in this book, so please, make both!

SERVES 6

1¼ lbs (563 g) beef stew meat

1½ tsp (8 g) salt, divided

½ tsp black pepper

¼ cup (30 g) all-purpose flour

4 tbsp (60 ml) olive oil, divided

1 medium green bell pepper, coarsely chopped

½ cup (75 g) diced yellow onion

1 (15-oz [420-g]) can Mexican corn, drained

2 cloves garlic, minced

2 to 3 chipotles in adobo

1 tbsp (9 g) chili powder

2 tsp (6 g) ground cumin

1 tsp smoked paprika

⅛ tsp ground cinnamon

1 (14½-oz [406-g]) can fire-roasted tomatoes, drained

1 medium sweet potato, peeled and diced

4 cups (960 ml) beef stock

Sliced jalapeños, for garnish

Tortilla chips, for garnish

Coarsely chopped fresh cilantro, for garnish

Lime wedges, for garnish

Place the beef in a medium bowl. Season the beef with 1 teaspoon of the salt and the black pepper. Add the flour and toss the beef to coat it.

Heat 2 tablespoons (30 ml) of the oil in a large, heavy-bottomed Dutch oven over medium-high heat. Add the beef and brown it on all sides, 4 to 5 minutes. Transfer the meat to a plate and set it aside.

Add the remaining 2 tablespoons (30 ml) of oil to the Dutch oven. Add the bell pepper, onion, corn, garlic and chipotles. Sauté for 5 to 7 minutes, or until the vegetables are soft. Season them with the chili powder, cumin, smoked paprika, remaining ½ teaspoon of salt and cinnamon.

Add the tomatoes, sweet potato and stock. Bring the mixture to a boil, reduce the heat to medium-low and cook for 15 minutes.

Garnish the stew with the jalapeños, tortilla chips, cilantro and lime wedges before serving.

Tomato-Pumpkin Soup with Pesto

There's nothing like breaking open a can of tomato soup and dunking that first bite of a grilled cheese into the soup—except we aren't breaking open any cans here. We're making our tomato-pumpkin soup from scratch, and let me tell you that this pairing is a match made in soup heaven! This soup is in my top five favorite recipes from this book, and I was blown away by the first bite. It's silky, smooth and packs a punch of smoky, roasted-tomato flavor you won't get out of a can.

SERVES 4

8 medium Roma tomatoes, seeded and quartered

6 cloves garlic, smashed

1 medium red bell pepper, seeded and quartered

1½ tsp (8 g) salt, divided

¼ tsp black pepper

3 tbsp (45 ml) olive oil

4 sprigs fresh thyme

1 (15-oz [420-g]) can pure pumpkin puree

1 tsp sugar

1 tsp smoked paprika

½ tsp ground cinnamon

2 cups (480 ml) vegetable stock

¼ cup (64 g) Homemade Pesto (page 35) or store-bought pesto

Preheat the oven to 400°F (204°C).

In a shallow, heavy-bottomed 6-quart (5.8-L) roasting pan that is also safe for the stovetop, combine the tomatoes, garlic, bell pepper, ½ teaspoon of the salt, black pepper, oil and thyme. Roast in the oven for 45 minutes, or until the vegetables are soft and charred.

Remove the roasting pan from the oven and allow the vegetables to cool slightly. Add the pumpkin, remaining 1 teaspoon of salt, sugar, smoked paprika, cinnamon and stock to the vegetables. Set the roasting pan over medium heat and bring the mixture to a simmer. Cook for 10 minutes.

Using an immersion blender, blend all the ingredients until they are smooth. If you do not have an immersion blender, you can let the ingredients cool, then carefully add them, in batches, to a countertop blender and blend until they are smooth. Use caution when following this method.

To serve, divide the soup into 4 bowls and top each with 1 tablespoon (16 g) of Homemade Pesto.

Beef Stew with Cheddar Dumplings

There was no way I was going to put a recipe for chicken and dumplings (page 10) in this book and not include a beef version for my meat-and-potatoes husband. This beef stew is rich and hearty, packed with vegetables and tender, flaky, cheesy dumplings to make the perfect comfort food.

SERVES 8

BEEF STEW

2 lbs (900 g) beef stew meat

1 tsp salt

½ tsp black pepper

½ cup (60 g) all-purpose flour

2 tbsp (30 ml) olive oil

2 tbsp (30 g) butter

5 cloves garlic, minced

1 cup (150 g) diced yellow onion

5 medium carrots, peeled and coarsely chopped

2 medium ribs celery, coarsely chopped

2 tbsp (30 ml) red wine vinegar

2 tbsp (34 g) tomato paste

1 (14½-oz [406-g]) can diced tomatoes, undrained

3 medium russet potatoes, peeled and diced

8 cups (1.9 L) beef stock

6 sprigs fresh thyme

2 dried bay leaves

CHEDDAR DUMPLINGS

2 cups (180 g) cake flour

2 tsp (8 g) baking powder

½ tsp salt

2 tbsp (30 g) butter

⅔ cup (160 ml) milk

2 tbsp (6 g) coarsely chopped fresh parsley

½ cup (60 g) shredded Cheddar cheese

(continued)

Beef Stew with Cheddar Dumplings (Continued)

To make the beef stew, place the beef in a large bowl and season it with the salt and black pepper. Add the flour and toss the beef to coat it.

Heat the oil in a 6.9-quart (6.6-L) heavy-bottomed Dutch oven over medium heat. Add the beef and brown it on all sides, 4 to 5 minutes. Transfer the beef to a plate and set it aside.

Add the butter to the Dutch oven and let it melt. Stir in the garlic, onion, carrots and celery. Sauté for 5 to 7 minutes, or until the vegetables are soft.

Stir in the vinegar and scrape up any bits from the bottom of the Dutch oven with a wooden spoon. Add the tomato paste and tomatoes.

Add the browned beef, potatoes, stock, thyme and bay leaves. Bring the stew to a boil, then reduce the heat to medium-low and cook for 45 to 60 minutes, or until the beef is tender.

Meanwhile, make the Cheddar dumplings. In a medium bowl, combine the cake flour, baking powder and salt. Cut the butter into the flour mixture and mix until coarse crumbs are formed. Slowly add the milk, stirring to combine. Fold in the parsley and Cheddar cheese.

When the beef is tender, add 1½-tablespoon (23-g) mounds of the dumpling dough to the surface of the stew. You should end up with approximately 16 dumplings. Cover the Dutch oven and simmer for 15 minutes, until the dumplings are fluffy. Discard the bay leaves.

Ladle the stew into individual bowls and top each serving with 2 dumplings.

Steak, Chicken and Sausage Gumbo

When brainstorming for this cookbook, I reached out to my best resource, my dad. He's a fantastic cook and someone from whom I get a lot of inspiration. This was one of the first recipes he suggested I develop, which makes sense. When it comes to rich, spicy, flavorful dishes, he knows what he's talking about and always delivers. As soon as I see him next, this is the very first dish I'll make him to show him just how much I appreciate him and all the things he's done for me, including encouraging me to create this book. Love you, Dad!

SERVES 6

½ cup (120 g) butter

¼ cup (60 ml) olive oil

1 cup (120 g) all-purpose flour

1 medium green bell pepper, coarsely chopped

1 medium yellow onion, diced

3 medium ribs celery, coarsely chopped

3 cloves garlic, minced

7 oz (196 g) Cajun andouille sausage, sliced into ½-inch (13-mm) rounds

1 (8-oz [224-g]) boneless, skinless chicken breast, cut into thin strips

8 oz (224 g) frozen grilled and seasoned beef steak strips

1 tsp Cajun seasoning

1 tsp salt

½ tsp black pepper

½ tsp smoked paprika

8 cups (1.9 L) beef or chicken stock

1 tbsp (15 ml) hot sauce

1 (15-oz [420-g]) can diced tomatoes, with liquid

1 (8-oz [248-ml]) can tomato sauce

2 dried bay leaves

1 tsp Worcestershire sauce

6 oz (168 g) frozen okra

Cooked white rice, for serving

3 green onions, thinly sliced, for garnish

(continued)

In a large Dutch oven over medium heat, combine the butter and oil. After the butter melts, stir in the flour to make a roux. Stirring constantly, cook the roux until it becomes a dark, rich brown color, 45 to 60 minutes.

Add the bell pepper, onion, celery and garlic to the roux and stir to combine. Add the sausage, chicken and steak. Cook for 10 minutes, or until the vegetables are tender. Stir in the Cajun seasoning, salt, black pepper and smoked paprika.

Add the stock, hot sauce, tomatoes, tomato sauce, bay leaves, Worcestershire sauce and okra. Bring the mixture to a boil, reduce the heat to medium-low and cook for 45 minutes.

Serve the gumbo over the rice and garnished with the green onions.

Beefy Peanut Butter Chili

When my girlfriend Kayla served me a peanut butter sandwich with a bowl of chili, I must have looked at her like she had two heads. "It's amazing," she declared. Curious, I dunked my sandwich into my chili and took a bite. It was life changing. I'm so happy I don't have to go the rest of my life without enjoying this combo. Now you don't have to either. For this chili, I skip the bread and add peanut butter directly to the mix. However, feel free to serve yourself an extra peanut butter sandwich on the side—I sure do!

SERVES 6

2 tbsp (30 ml) olive oil, divided

1 lb (450 g) ground beef

1 medium green bell pepper, coarsely chopped

1 medium yellow onion, diced

2 cloves garlic, minced

1 medium jalapeño, seeded and diced

2 tbsp (18 g) chili powder

2 tbsp (18 g) ground cumin

1 tbsp (3 g) dried oregano

1 tsp salt

½ tsp black pepper

¼ tsp ground cinnamon

8 oz (224 g) tomato paste

½ cup (90 g) smooth peanut butter

1 tbsp (15 ml) Worcestershire sauce

1 (15-oz [420-g]) can no-sodium diced tomatoes, undrained

3 cups (720 ml) beef stock

1 (15-oz [420-g]) can pinto beans, drained and rinsed

Thinly sliced green onions for garnish (optional)

Heat 1 tablespoon (15 ml) of the oil in a large Dutch oven over medium-high heat. Add the beef, breaking it up into an even layer. Allow it to brown for 5 minutes on one side before stirring. Flip the meat over and cook for 5 minutes more.

Push the meat off to one side of the Dutch oven and add the remaining 1 tablespoon (15 ml) of oil. Add the bell pepper, onion, garlic and jalapeño. Sauté for 5 minutes, or until the vegetables are soft and mixed with the beef. Season the mixture with the chili powder, cumin, oregano, salt, black pepper and cinnamon. Stir in the tomato paste and peanut butter and cook for 1 to 2 minutes, or until they are incorporated.

Add the Worcestershire sauce, tomatoes and stock and simmer for 30 minutes. Stir in the beans and cook for 10 minutes before serving. Top with green onions, if using.

Chicken, Broccoli and Rice Soup

Remember the chicken, broccoli and rice casserole you ate on a weekly basis when you were growing up? This recipe is exactly that, but in a cheesy, creamy soup. It's perfect for a chilly night or to send to someone who needs a little extra comfort.

SERVES 6

4 tbsp (60 ml) olive oil, divided

1 lb (450 g) boneless, skinless chicken breasts, diced

½ tsp salt

¼ tsp black pepper

½ cup (75 g) diced onion

2 cloves garlic, minced

¼ cup (30 g) all-purpose flour

2 cups (480 ml) milk

4 cups (960 ml) chicken stock

1 cup (210 g) long-grain white rice

1 to 2 cups (175 to 350 g) broccoli florets

1 cup (120 g) shredded Cheddar cheese

Heat 2 tablespoons (30 ml) of the oil in a medium pot over medium heat. Add the chicken and season it with the salt and black pepper. Cook the chicken until it is browned on all sides, 8 to 10 minutes. Transfer the chicken to a plate and set it aside.

Add the remaining 2 tablespoons (30 ml) of oil to the pot. Add the onion and garlic and cook for 5 minutes, or until they are soft. Stir in the flour and cook for 1 minute.

Slowly whisk in the milk and stock. Bring the mixture to a boil. Add the rice, reduce the heat to medium-low and cook for 10 minutes.

Stir in the chicken, broccoli and Cheddar cheese and cook for 5 minutes.

Beer Brat Corn Chowder

Being from the Midwest, we eat brats often. We also love our cheese, so it's a no-brainer that we'd combine them in a soup and then add corn too. The result is a creamy soup that's perfect for crisp fall nights and game days.

SERVES 6

2 tbsp (30 g) butter

1 cup (165 g) fresh or frozen corn

½ cup (75 g) diced onion

3 cloves garlic, minced

1 medium jalapeño, seeded and diced

⅓ cup (40 g) all-purpose flour

½ tsp dried oregano

½ tsp smoked paprika

½ tsp salt

¼ tsp black pepper

12 oz (360 ml) American light lager–style beer (see note)

3 cups (720 ml) beef stock

½ cup (120 ml) half-and-half

19 oz (532 g) beer brats, sliced into ½-inch (13-mm) rounds

2 cups (240 g) shredded sharp white Cheddar cheese, divided

2 green onions, finely chopped

Melt the butter in a large pot over medium heat. Add the corn and sauté for 5 minutes. Add the onion, garlic and jalapeño and cook for 10 minutes, until the vegetables are soft.

Sprinkle in the flour, oregano, smoked paprika, salt and black pepper.

Slowly whisk in the beer, stock and half-and-half. Bring the mixture to a boil. Add the brats, reduce the heat to low and cook for 10 minutes.

Add 1½ cups (180 g) of the Cheddar cheese and cook until it melts into the soup.

To serve, divide the soup among individual bowls and top each serving with green onions and some of the remaining ½ cup (60 g) of Cheddar cheese.

NOTE: If you prefer not to use beer, feel free to use 1½ cups (360 ml) of beef stock or water.

Chicken Noodle Pho

Traditionally, pho is made with beef, but I opt for chicken. This version reminds me of chicken noodle soup, which I always crave as soon as there's a slight nip in the air. The aromatic spices are so fragrant in this sped-up classic that you'll instantly fall in love with it.

SERVES 4

CHICKEN NOODLE PHO

1 (3-inch [8-cm]) piece fresh ginger, peeled and thinly sliced

3 green onions, sliced into 2-inch (5-cm) pieces

1 medium bunch fresh cilantro

6 whole cloves

4 star anise pods

2 (3- to 4-inch [8- to 10-cm]) cinnamon sticks

2 cardamom pods

1 tbsp (8 g) black peppercorns

1 tbsp (5 g) coriander seeds

4 cups (960 ml) chicken stock

2 cups (480 ml) water

1 lb (450 g) boneless, skinless chicken breasts

4 oz (112 g) rice noodles

TOPPINGS

Bean sprouts

Coarsely chopped fresh cilantro

Lime wedges

Sliced jalapeños

Coarsely chopped fresh mint

Coarsely chopped fresh basil

In a medium Dutch oven over medium heat, combine the ginger, green onions and cilantro. Slightly mash the ingredients with the end of a wooden spoon.

Lay the cloves, star anise, cinnamon, cardamom, peppercorns and coriander on a piece of cheesecloth. Tie up the cheesecloth to make a bag and place it in the Dutch oven. Pour in the stock and water and bring the mixture to a simmer. Add the chicken and bring the mixture to a boil. Cook for 15 to 20 minutes, or until the chicken's internal temperature reaches 165°F (74°C). Turn off the heat and transfer the chicken to a cutting board. When it is cool enough to handle, shred the chicken. Add the rice noodles to warm stock water and soak until pliable, about 15 minutes, and drain.

Pour the broth in the Dutch oven through a strainer into a large bowl and return the liquid to the Dutch oven. Discard the solids. Transfer the chicken and rice noodles back to the Dutch oven and stir them into the broth.

Divide the soup among 4 bowls and top each serving with the bean sprouts, cilantro, lime wedges, jalapeños, mint and basil.

Cheesy Smoked Ham and Wild Rice Soup

This creamy soup is based off the classic chicken and wild rice soup, but I jazzed things up with some smoky ham and cheese. This soup is creamy, comforting and packed with delicious vegetables. It would be the perfect dish to make after the holidays if you have any leftover ham.

SERVES 6

4 tbsp (60 g) butter

2 cloves garlic, minced

1 cup (150 g) diced yellow onion

3 medium carrots, peeled and coarsely chopped

3 medium ribs celery, coarsely chopped

3 sprigs fresh thyme

¼ cup (30 g) all-purpose flour

4 cups (960 ml) chicken stock

2 cups (480 ml) water

1 lb (450 g) smoked ham, cubed

1 cup (144 g) wild rice

2 cups (480 ml) heavy cream or half-and-half

1 cup (120 g) grated Cheddar cheese

Crusty baguettes, for serving

Melt the butter in a large Dutch oven over medium heat. Add the garlic, onion, carrots, celery and thyme and sauté until the vegetables are soft, 5 to 7 minutes.

Stir in the flour and cook for 1 minute.

Slowly whisk in the stock and water.

Add the ham and rice. Bring the mixture to a boil, reduce the heat to medium-low and cook for 40 to 45 minutes, or until the rice is tender.

Remove the soup from the heat and stir in the cream and Cheddar cheese.

Ladle the soup into serving bowls and serve with the baguettes.

ACKNOWLEDGMENTS

TO MY HUSBAND, JIM, thank you for believing in me and inspiring me to write this book, sampling all of my food (the good, the bad and the ugly) and for putting up with my crazy antics throughout this whole process. It was because you believed in me that this book came to fruition. I love you most!

TO A AND C, thank you for letting me finish "just this one recipe" before heading off to swim in the pool, play in the park or just hang out. I appreciate your patience and love you both more than chocolate cake!

TO MY DAD, for your encouraging words phone call after phone call (and there were a lot). Those "go kick some butt" and "you've got this" pep talks pushed me when I didn't think I could look at one more clove of garlic. I appreciate and love you more than you'll ever know, and I'm so blessed to call you Dad.

TO MY MOM AND MY SISTER, without you two, I don't know where I would be in this life. Thank you for always being there for me. Love you!

TO MY GIRL TRIBE, thank you for always being my biggest cheerleaders and empowering me to finish this book. You rock. Love you!

TO MY #MM, I'm so happy to have met you. Our weekly phone calls, emails and texts always lift my spirits and motivate me to keep going. Thank you for your support!

TO CAITLIN AND PAGE STREET PUBLISHING, thank you for that first email that got this entire project off the ground. It is because of you that I am holding a published cookbook in my hands, a dream I never thought possible.

Last but not least, thank you to my READERS OF STRAWBERRY BLONDIE KITCHEN. You are the number one reason I am here today. Thank you from the bottom of my heart!

ABOUT THE AUTHOR

MEGAN MARLOWE is the founder of the food blog Strawberry Blondie Kitchen, where she creates everyday recipes for the whole family. Her recipes have been featured on BuzzFeed, *Cosmopolitan*, Kraft Foods and MSN.com. She lives in Illinois with her husband, two children and dog. She runs on the three Cs: caffeine, craft beer and cheese (in no particular order). She hopes to inspire her readers to get into the kitchen and create amazing dishes, all while enjoying themselves. After all, cooking should be fun!

INDEX